PUEBLO MOTHERS AND CHILDREN

PUEBLO MOTHERS AND CHILDREN:

Essays by Elsie Clews Parsons, 1915-1924

edited by

Barbara A. Babcock

Ancient City Press
Santa Fe, New Mexico

Standard Book Number:
Clothbound 0-941270-66-1
Paperback 0-941270-65-3
Library of Congress Catalogue Number: 89-082082

First Edition

Designed by Don Curry

Frontisepiece Photograph: Pablita Chauarria of Santa Clara Pueblo.
Photograph by T. Harmon Parkhurst, 1925.
Courtesy of the Museum of New Mexico.
Negative number 4206.

All photographs in this edition are reproduced courtesy of the Museum of New Mexico and the American Philosophical Society.

"Zuñi Conception and Pregnancy Beliefs" is reprinted courtesy of the International Congress of Americanists.

"Nativity Myth at Laguna and Zuñi" is reprinted courtesy of the *Journal of American Folklore.*

"Waiyautitsa of Zuñi, New Mexico" and "Getting Married on First Mesa, Arizona" are reprinted courtesy of *Science.*

"Increase by Magic: A Zuñi Pattern" and "The Zuñi La'mana" are reprinted courtesy of the *American Anthropologist.*

"Mothers and Children at Laguna," "Mothers and Children at Zuñi, New Mexico," "Hopi Mothers and Children," "Tewa Mothers and Children" are reprinted courtesy of *Man.*

for my mother, Harriett Horning Babcock
1914-1989

for Helen Cordero, the Pueblo woman who has shared
her home and her life with me

for Marsie, Marta, Beverly, Carmen, Jan, Shirley, Susan, and Barbie
southwestern mothers, sisters, friends

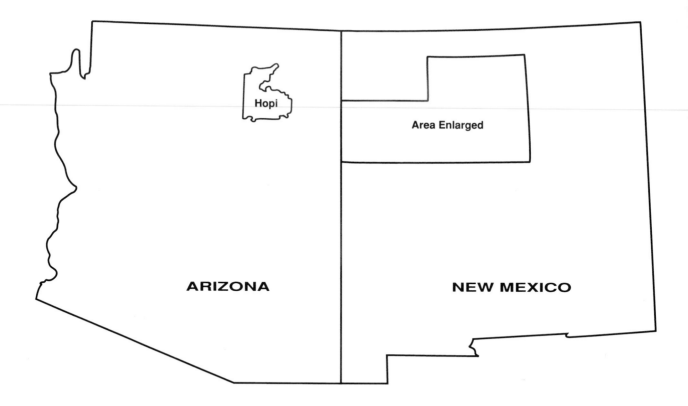

Hopi

Area Enlarged

ARIZONA

NEW MEXICO

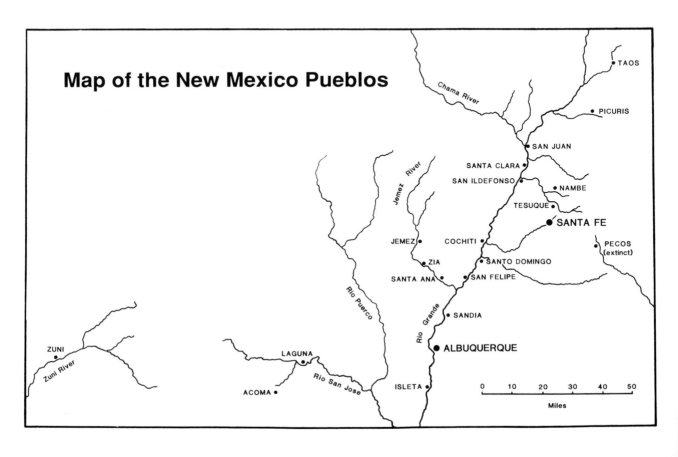

Map of the New Mexico Pueblos

Chama River

• TAOS

• PICURIS

• SAN JUAN

SANTA CLARA •

SAN ILDEFONSO •

• NAMBE

TESUQUE •

● SANTA FE

JEMEZ • COCHITI •

PECOS
(extinct) •

ZIA •

SANTO DOMINGO •

SANTA ANA • SAN FELIPE •

• SANDIA

● ALBUQUERQUE

ZUNI •

LAGUNA •

ACOMA •

ISLETA •

Jemez River

Rio Puerco

Rio Grande

Zuni River

Rio San Jose

0   10   20   30   40   50

Miles

Contents

Preface
ix

Introduction
Elsie Clews Parsons and the Pueblo Construction of Gender
1

Elsie Clews Parsons' Essays on Pueblo Mothers and Children

Preface

I first began reading Elsie Clews Parsons in 1976 when I contemplated doing field research on Pueblo clowning. Her anthropological work was presented to me as necessary medicine—indispensable but unpleasant. I dreaded having, as I was told, "to slug [my] way through Parsons." What I discovered was not at all the dry, atheoretical compendia that I expected, and I began to look forward to those evenings when I could escape from reading, teaching, and writing about literature into *Pueblo Indian Religion* (1939). The more I read of this "monumental," two-volume contribution that is the culmination of her twenty-five years of Pueblo research, the more fascinated I became, not only with the intricacies of Pueblo religion, cosmology and social organization but with the woman who devoted so much of her life to understanding it.

Who was this woman who contributed so much time, energy and money to American folklore and anthropology and supported the work of other Southwest scholars, especially the female students of Franz Boas? Histories of southwestern anthropology told me little about the women who have worked in the region and contributed to our understanding of its indigenous peoples, even one so prolific and influential as Parsons. The realization of that gap in our understanding led in 1984 to *Daughters of the Desert,* a multi-faceted recuperative and revisionary project concerning women anthropologists, that I co-organized with Nancy Parezo.

In the meantime, as my own Pueblo research developed and I began working with Cochiti potter Helen Cordero, creator of the Storyteller doll, I became preoccupied with the the dynamics of the reproduction of culture and with the idea of reproduction in Pueblo culture. Here too Parsons provided invaluable insights, and it was then that I first encountered and came to appreciate the articles collected in this volume. These essays, engendered by her relationships with Pueblo women and her concern with the cultural construction of maternity, deserve a wider audience in anthropology and feminist scholarship.

For over a decade now Elsie has been a constant companion in many respects, especially since I started working with her papers in 1985. I got to know her better by reading letters and fieldnotes and unpublished manuscripts, and began to understand the feminist and pacifist and the mother and wife and lover behind the intrepid anthropologist. Her energy, her productivity, her generosity, her courage, and most of all her integrity were astonishing, are inspiring. Her "unflinching" "un-compromisingness" was buttressed by wealth and status, and she was indomitable. While I may joke that "when I grow up I want to be Elsie Clews Parsons," I can say in all seriousness that there has been more than one occasion in the past five years when her example and her work have given me strength and kept me going.

This book is a case in point. It was conceived in the months of my mother's dying, and it was always there as something that I wanted to work on rather than one of the many things I had to do. That it should have taken priority among several Parsons projects in process, especially after I was told that I would never have children myself, is not surprising. While Elsie dealt with her problems by taking a train to Gallup and immersing herself in Pueblo research, I came to terms with my losses these past months largely by rereading and writing about her work on Pueblo mothers and children. Other studies I have done have been more difficult, more time-consuming, or more important professionally, but with the exception of my relationship with Helen Cordero, none has been more meaningful or more sustaining.

Therefore, my thanks, first of all, to Elsie Clews Parsons, who continues to support southwestern research and contribute to our understanding of Pueblo life. Without Marta Weigle, Mary Powell and Ancient City Press this book would have never happened. I am immensely grateful to them for their support, their efforts on behalf of *Pueblo Mothers and Children* and their firm and gentle prodding when, for all the aforementioned reasons, it was hard to let go of this project. Beth Carroll Horrocks of the American Philosophical Society Library and Arthur Olivas of the Museum of New Mexico Photo Archives have been consistently helpful. I am indebted to them and to their institutions for the illustrations that accompany this text. Jay Cox has been an indispensable and incomparable research assistant, running down obscure references, expediting interlibrary loans, and recopying Parsons essays at twice their original size. Finally and most importantly, my thanks to Kit Hinsley who has loved and inspired, criticized and supported, and shared much of the archival research. Mutual discoveries, spring lunches on Independence Mall, and shivering winter walks through Philadelphia streets gave new meaning to dusty work. I couldn't have done it without him.

Introduction:

ELSIE CLEWS PARSONS AND THE PUEBLO CONSTRUCTION OF GENDER

So generation succeeds generation, the slow stream of
mothers and daughters forming a current that carried with it
husbands, sons, and grandsons.

A.L. Kroeber, Zuñi Kin and Clan*, 1917*

Women anthropologists have as women a necessary
function in the investigation of influences brought to bear
upon the child. Equally, they have a necessary function in
investigating the adjustment of women in different cultures.
Most anthropological accounts are written from the men's
angle; the native women remain unknown quantities.

Ruth Benedict, "Women and Anthropology," *1940*

Feminist, sociologist, anthropologist, folklorist, wife, mother, fieldworker, socialite, Elsie Clews Parsons (1874-1941) resists easy categorization. Both her life and her work have been "characterized by a strenuous revolt against convention."[1] Whether writing as a feminist sociologist, as a folklorist or as an anthropologist, Parsons was preoccupied throughout her career with the relationship between cultural formations and the constitution of the subject, especially the female subject. The real interest of Elsie Clews Parsons' writing is to be found in the interstices between her feminist questioning and anthropological research. The essays collected in this volume attest that Parsons' feminism definitely informed her Pueblo ethnology in its concern with the cultural construction of gender, sexuality, and reproduction—with motherhood as experience, as discourse and as institution.[2]

The society matron with her first child. Elsie Clews Parsons with her daughter Lissa in 1900. Photograph courtesy of the American Philosophical Society.

Elsie Clews Parsons discovered the Southwest in 1910. She returned in 1912 and 1913 on ethnographic reconnaissance trips and initially contemplated doing archaeology at Puye Cliffs. In August 1915, at the age of forty-one, she began doing fieldwork in Zuñi. That year she also published the first of countless essays in the *American Anthropologist* and presented her first paper on Zuñi at the 19th Congress of Americanists. Not insignificantly, it concerned "Zuñi Conception and Pregnancy Beliefs" [1, reprinted below]. A regular contributor to *The Masses* and *The New Republic,* she also published twenty-seven notes, articles and reviews in 1915 on such feminist and pacifist subjects as "Marriage and the Will to Power" and "Anti-suffragists and the War," as well as *Social Freedom,* her fifth volume of feminist sociology.

In 1916 Parsons published no less than seven articles on Zuñi, more than twice that number on feminist and pacifist issues and her sixth and last feminist monograph, *Social Rule.* It was this pattern of scholarly productivity that led Pliny Earle Goddard to tease her that year about doing "research in the summer" and writing "propaganda in the winter." Alfred L. Kroeber joked about her "provocative books" and addressed her as "Dear Propagandist," but in response to one of her first essays on Zuñi, he lamented: "I wish we could write *our* anthropology as well as you do." Robert Lowie similarly taunted her and finally she wrote to him in 1916: "You, Kroeber, and [A. M.] Hocart make the life of a psychologist not worth living. I see plainly I shall have to keep to the straight and narrow path of kinship nomenclature and folktale collecting."[3] Instead, Parsons gave up the publication of generalizing ethnology concerned with such cultural universals as "aversions to anomalies", and her explicitly feminist and pacifist texts. By 1920 her published scholarship consisted almost entirely of Pueblo ethnography and Afro-American folktales.

The influence of Goddard, Kroeber, and Lowie as well as Franz Boas *was* profound, and it is tempting to attribute this turn in her research and writing solely to a desire to conform to masculine discursive standards of scientific anthropology.[4] Undoubtedly that was a factor, but her unpublished materials reveal other compelling reasons. World War I crushed Parsons' radical hopes for progress and reform and created ruptures within her family and her intellectual circle. Even after her husband enlisted and her friends deserted the cause, she persisted in her pacifism. Increasingly, however, her essays against the war were rejected. Between 1914 and 1921, no less than forty-five manuscripts dealing with feminist and pacifist subjects were "declined."[5] During the same time all of her fieldwork-based essays submitted to folklore and anthropological journals were accepted for publication. Whatever factors drew her toward ethnographic research and writing, discursive politics surely pushed her in that direction. In 1917 she wrote to Kroeber: "Life for a militant pacifist has been rather trying these past months and if I hadn't my Zuñi notes to write up and no end of Negro folk tales to edit—I'd be worse off than I am."[6]

Finally, personal factors influenced Parsons' turn to anthropological fieldwork in 1915. Several years before Elsie not only lost a child but discovered a serious affair on her husband Herbert's part. Prior to doing field research her response was to take an increasing number of trips with other men. "The only alternative," she wrote to Herbert, "was staying home with you depressed and so repressed that I know that at any moment I might be very disagreeable in all sorts of unreasonable ways."[7] The war left the already estranged couple little common ground. Anthropology, with its combination of adventure, hard work, and sense of mission, engaged her emotionally as well as intellectually and physically, resolved a midlife crisis and offered legitimate escape.

Parsons escaped indeed to the Southwest, often several times in one year between 1915 and 1925. She savored the beauty of the landscape and flourished in the opportunity fieldwork provided both to have an identity and to be transformed by another people:[8]

> This cave room faced south and that night I looked out from its frame on the moonlit talus below and the pines beyond and thought that whether Indian or White one was fortunate indeed to live for a time in a world of such beauty. . . . If ever I come to work seriously in this country I suspect that it will not be as an archaeologist, but as a student of the culture of today. It is interesting to reconstruct the culture of the ancient town builders, but it is still more interesting to study the minds and ways of their descendents.[9]

In the words of her mother, the southwestern transformation that began this first night spent at Puye Cliffs was "scandalous." Daughter Lissa described how Elsie would return to New York "looking perfectly dreadful, a bandanna around her hair, and her disreputable saddlebags full of manuscripts."[10] Parsons' fieldnotes, letters and both published and unpublished essays attest that she loved the adventure, established unusually close friendships with her Pueblo hosts and hostesses, had her hair washed at Hopi in 1920, and cherished the gift of an Indian name and identity. She continued to correspond with and send gifts to her Pueblo friends after she returned to New York.

For Parsons as for other radical and disaffected women of her time, issues of race, ethnicity and class came to stand in for gender; feminism was transformed into a preoccupation with other cultures, other differences and inequalities, and an advocacy of cultural relativism. However, even if explicitly expressed only in the footnotes of her later ethnological writings, Parsons never forgot that she was both a woman and a feminist. Her gender and her politics shaped both the substance and the style of her anthropology, influencing what she studied, whom she talked to and how she wrote about it in both published and unpublished contexts. Not surprisingly, she carried her earlier concerns with the cultural and psychological roots of sexual identity into her fieldwork, arguing not only that ethnology could help women but that women could aid ethnology, for "a woman student would have many opportunities for observing the life of women and children that male ethnographers have lacked."[11]

Parsons' own wisdom coincided with the advice Kroeber gave her when she followed him to Zuni in 1915: "You could do no better, if you propose staying for more than a day, than to lay your plans before [Governor Lewis's] wife, who is an educated Cherokee, and ask her advice how to carry them out." Parsons did so, and the result was an intimate relationship and an important anthropological collaboration. In her first letter to Herbert from Zuni, she described her situation and Margaret Lewis as follows:

> This place a huge success, so I'm staying here all my time and not going on to the Hopi country. Staying in Governor's house where Kroeber stayed. The woman is an extremely educated Cherokee, once a schoolteacher here and she is a great help. The valley is glorious!"[12]

Parsons' Zuni field notebooks from 1915 contain long sections on childbearing and on "occupation by sex" based both on her observations and her conversations with Margaret Lewis; "Zuñi Conception and Pregnancy Beliefs" was the first of several academic presentations and publications resulting from this collaborative research. "In the Southwest," her unpublished essays from this period, also reveal a preoccupation with the gender division of labor and a focus on women's activities as well as profound respect for Margaret Lewis.[13]

On horseback in New Mexico near Santa Clara Pueblo in 1912 or 1913 in her "unconventional" field attire. Elsie's hostess, Clara True, described in "In the Southwest," "much disapproved of [her] habits of smoking and wearing riding-breeches." Photograph courtesy of the American Philosophical Society.

Parsons' initial concern with other ways of being female continued throughout her Pueblo research. In each pueblo where she worked during the following decade, Parsons established close relationships with women and collected material on mothers and children and on the pragmatics and symbolics of reproduction. While it might be argued, as Louise Lamphere and others have,[14] that Parsons' early anthropology involves little more than a continuation of the focus on women's roles and search for universals in women's experience that characterized her feminist sociology, it should be emphasized here that both Parsons' feminist sociology and her Pueblo ethnology demonstrate a much more complicated concern with the cultural construction of gender and sexuality—with what she termed "classification by sex" and with the maternal body as an object of control.

Margaret Lewis, Parsons' Zuni friend, hostess, and consultant. Photograph courtesy of Desert Magazine.

Unlike many feminists of her own and later generations, Parsons did not regard maternity and feminism as mutually exclusive choices either practically or theoretically.[15] While teaching, researching and writing, she gave birth to six children, four of whom lived to adulthood, and repeatedly advocated that maternity be improved through the mother's education and occupation outside the home. In both her sociology and her anthropology Parsons recognized, as Julia Kristeva and others have much more recently, that "the mother's body, her desire, and her status, meaning, and power within culture are of central importance to any discussion of the socio-symbolic, signifying order"—that "maternity is the unspoken foundation of all social and signifying relations,"[16] and that this "universal" and "essential" experience is in turn culturally configured and locally elaborated. Just as surely as recent feminist critiques in anthropology have, Parsons challenged the "naturalness" of mothering, both theoretically in her sociology and empirically in her studies of Pueblo culture, documenting "how the category 'woman' is linked to such attributes of motherhood as fertility, naturalness, maternal love, nurturance, life-giving and reproduction."[17]

Parsons' essays such as "Zuñi Conception and Pregnancy Beliefs" (1915), "Increase by Magic: A Zuñi Pattern" (1919), and "Nativity Myth at Laguna and Zuñi" (1918) give substance and detail to H. K. Haeberlin's generalizations concerning the importance of "the idea of fertilization" on which "almost every [Pueblo] cultural phenomenon seems to be focused." In describing the conception beliefs associated with rabbit and deer hunting and the interconnections among animal, vegetable and human fertility in "Zuñi Conception and Pregnancy Beliefs" she too recognized that reproduction is the root metaphor or key symbol of Pueblo culture. However, in contrast to Haeberlin's monolithic characterization of Pueblo culture, Parsons was preoccupied with the differences as well as commonalities concerning reproductive beliefs and practices among the Pueblo villages she studied.[18] In addition to discussing increase as the ideological focus of Pueblo life, Parsons recognized that continuity over time is a political and symbolic as well as a biological matter.

Given her understanding of motherhood as "a cultural construction which different societies build up and elaborate in different ways,"[19] she was particularly interested in culture contact and the ways in which the Virgin Mary and Nativity myth were incorporated into Pueblo rituals of increase. In "Nativity Myth" she describes how the *santu* is "put into the pattern of Zuñi fetiches . . . [and] like them, is a source of light in the sense of life." Rites of increase are similarly associated with both winter solstice ceremonial and Christmas. Parsons discusses this convergence of Pueblo and Spanish practices in "Increase by Magic", noting that on the sixth day of the prayer stick planting associated with the winter solstice, "the saint begins to lie in *(santu chalia*, saint, childbirth) for four days." This attention to the consequences of acculturation and to the pragmatics of Pueblo cultural survival not only reflects Franz Boas's preoccupation with cultural dynamics at the time Parsons was associated with him, but stands in marked contrast to the ahistorical essentialism and romantic primitivism characteristic of Frank Hamilton Cushing on "primitive motherhood" and H. K. Haeberlin on "the idea of fertilization" among Pueblo peoples.[20]

Parsons' analyses of the Pueblo construction of gender also differ markedly from traditional kinship studies which consider reproduction only indirectly in terms of family and social organization. Her perspective that these kin and clan relations are inseparable from ideas of reproduction and that kinship and marriage are, in turn, what Henrietta L. Moore calls "powerful determinants of the way in which ideas about gender are constructed" is evident in *Laguna Genealogies* (1923), which includes over twenty pages on marriage, sexuality and reproduction in addition to genealogies and kinship data. In *Notes on Zuñi, Pt. 2* (1917), Parsons is concerned with kinship "in ceremonialism" such as kin duties associated with birth, again anticipating contemporary feminist anthropologists who see gender constructs as highly "ritualized statements" which not only reflect social relationships but elaborate on salient social and political concerns. Without a doubt, she would have agreed with her colleague Bronislaw Malinowski, who later argued that in each culture motherhood is "a relationship specific to that culture...and correlated to the whole social structure of the community. This means that the problem of maternity cannot be dismissed as a zoological fact...the theory of cultural motherhood should have been made the foundation of a general theory of kinship."[21]

The four essays on Pueblo "Mothers and Children" (Laguna, Zuni, Hopi, and Tewa) that Parsons published in *Man* between 1919 and 1924 are important not only for the intertextual comparisons and contrasts she makes among different pueblos, but for her specific and general concerns with the consequences of acculturation on beliefs and practices associated with marriage, pregnancy and child rearing. Her description of the "little boy" made by her Hopi "sister" to ensure the birth of a male child and kept in the back room with her ceremonial things, which turns out to be not a kachina but "an out-and-out American doll," is a particularly interesting example. Parsons also paid specific attention to female sexuality, reproduction and sex roles in each of her Pueblo monographs. No less than thirty pages of *The Social Organization of the Tewa* (1929) is devoted to these concerns and her final and most controversial Pueblo community study, *Taos Pueblo* (1936), includes sections on "Adolescence of Girls," "Restriction in Marriage Choices," "Illegitimacy: Prostitution" and "Courtship and Marriage."

Clearly, Parsons' preoccupation with marriage did not end when she stopped writing feminist sociology; neither was it confined to the ethnographic description of marriage practices. Even in her collections of Pueblo folktales Parsons focuses on courtship and marriage customs, as in her introduction to *Tewa Tales* (1926), where she compares the Tewa of the Rio Grande with the Hopi-Tewa of First Mesa among whom she had worked in 1920. In discussing the influence of the anthropologist's interests on the nature of the tales told by Pueblo narrators she recalls "that wedding minutiae would get into almost every tale of the First Mesa narrator who knew I was interested in Hopi weddings."[22] That narrator may have been Yellow-pine, the Tewa woman whose narrative of wedding practices is published as it was told to Parsons in "Getting Married on First Mesa, Arizona" (1921), juxtaposed with another account by a Tewa man which reveals "the extent of Hopi elaboration" on Tewa practices. At the conclusion of the latter's narrative Parsons asks: "When is the first time they sleep together?" He replies,

'The night of the morning they wash the girl's head. I forgot that.' He forgot that, because, I presume, it was the ceremonial that was of significance, not the personal relationship. 'I forgot that'—what more telling comment on wedding ceremonial—anywhere?

Parsons' preoccupation with gender and sexuality as culturally constructed is explicit early and late in two essays about Zuni transvestism, "The Zuñi La'mana" (1916) and "The Last Zuñi Transvestite" (1939). The first is reprinted here; the second is a note based on a 1938 report by John Adair about Kasinelu, one of the four transvestites she described in 1916, who, she suggests, "will almost certainly be the last one" because "American influence will work against the trait." Long interested in classification and anomalousness, Parsons was fascinated by the *la'mana* and what she considered the "feminist nature" of Pueblo culture.[23] Accepted both as lifelong behavioral patterns and as temporary ritual burlesque, such "men-women" throw into sharp relief expectations and values which Pueblo culture associates with being female, challenge the "naturalness" of sex differences and make a reflexive commentary on gender ideology. When she asked for local reasons and explanations, Parsons was told "that the person in question made the change because he wanted to work like a woman or because his household was short of women and needed a woman worker." And, always attuned to the uses of anthropology as cultural critique, she glosses:

This native theory of the institution of the man-woman is a curious commentary, is it not, on that thorough-going belief in the intrinsic difference between the sexes which is so tightly held to in our own culture?[24]

Parsons poses this rhetorical question at the end of her most interesting and most complete portrait of the Pueblo woman, "Waiyautitsa of Zuñi". This fictive biography of a Zuni woman was written for a popular audience and originally published in *Scientific Monthly* in 1919. Later hailed by Clyde Kluckhohn as the first Southwest study of culture and personality,[25] this sketch was the impetus for *American Indian Life* (1922), a collection of portraits of Native Americans written by anthropologists on the basis of ethnographic facts and edited by Parsons for a popular

A typical entry in one of the notebooks Elsie used for fieldwork and carried in her saddlebags. This describes one of her first days in Laguna and exemplifies her pattern of working with women and focusing on women's matters. Courtesy of the American Philosophical Society.

audience. Her stated aim was to counteract the stereotypes of Fenimore Cooper, introduce the public to the richness and diversity of American Indian life and produce something "for a girl to read who is going to spend her life among Indians." The result, according to Leslie Spier, was

> something of a minor triumph in seeing that we acknowledged that a culture is the sum of the cultures of individuals and that their personal problems represent the adjustment of desires to the framework of habit and convention. The book thus marks a turning point from earlier normalized accounts to ethnographies full-blooded with the records of individual participation. Her own reports, especially, in the years that followed, are replete with such material.[26]

What Spier does not say is that Parsons was particularly interested in women as persons and, in that respect, this essay may also be regarded as something of a benchmark in feminist anthropology. Certainly this is the earliest essay of which I am aware demonstrating that "an enquiry into the cultural construction of self or person, through an analysis of gender identity, is an area where feminist anthropology [can] make a significant and substantial contribution to theoretical development within the discipline."[27]

"Waiyautitsa" is also noteworthy in being one of very few anthropological publications in which Parsons is explicit about her feminism, beginning with the sentence, "Only twice through my association with Pueblo Indians has it occurred to me to be a feminist." The first time was at Cochiti, when her hostess grumbled about having to stay up to feed her husband when he returned from the kiva. The second was when she was asked to write an article on Zuni women for *The American Museum Journal* of the American Museum of Natural History. This essay, which subsequently became "Waiyautitsa," was rejected "because it contained a reference to the lack of prostitution at Zuñi." Wryly acknowledging the romantic primitivism characteristic of popular anthropological presentation, Parsons adds:

> Recognition of the subject was considered unsuitable for boy and girl readers; it was deemed better for them to have a partial survey of the facts of life than to see life whole, even at Zuñi. Nor was life at Zuñi to suggest inquiry into life at home.[28]

In the version of the essay published in *American Indian Life* these very revealing opening paragraphs were deleted and replaced with the following much more conventional and evocative "approach" characteristic of travel writing.[29] However, at the same time that she contributes to the anthropological romance of Zuni, Parsons deconstructs the superior vantage point of the civilized anthropologist such as Cushing or her male companion at this later moment, presumably Kroeber, looking down on the simplicities of primitive life:

> 'Isn't it hard to believe that life should be so intricate and complex among those meek, adobe houses on that low hill?'
>
> We were on the last mile or so of the forty-mile drive through the red sandstone above and below, and the green cedar and spruce and sagebrush from Gallup to Zuñi; behind us to the southeast was the great mesa to which three centuries ago the people had escaped for a while from Spanish arrogance, the mesa where one day we were to seek for the shrines of the War Leaders and the Song Youth and the Earth Woman as we ostensibly hunted rabbits; and before us, barely in sight, so quietly does an Indian pueblo fit into the landscape, were the rectangular blocks of the many-stories Zuñi houses whose flat roofs make broken lines, mesa-like, against the sky. At the highest point, a three-storied house, the town crier was probably at that very moment calling out to the townspeople the orders of the governor and council for the following day; but we were still too far away to hear, quiet as was the air, and our unarrested eyes turned westward to the flaming spectacle of a sunset the like of which is not to be seen outside the sweeping valley plain of Zuñi.
>
> Now and again, as you walk between those 'meek, adobe houses,' dodging a snouting pig, or assuming indifference to the dogs that dash out from every corner to snarl or yelp; now and again as you see the villagers going about their daily affairs, men driving in from the fields, or taking the horses in or out of the corrals, women fetching water from the well or bound on a visit to a neighbor, little boys chasing one another and babies playing about in the dirt, now and again that first impression of material simplicity returns and with it the feeling that the round of life must be simple, too. But the feeling never lasts long, never holds its own with the crowding impressions of ceremonial rain dance or pilgrimage or domiciliary visitation, of baffling sacerdotal organi-

zation and still more baffling sacerdotal feuds, of elaborate pantheon, of innumerable myths and tales, of associations in story or cult with every hill and rock and spring, of kinship ramifications and matrimonial histories, of irksome relationships with Mexicans and 'Americans,' and of village gossip which is made up so comprehensively of the secular and sacred as to pass far beyond the range of even a New England church social.

Is it not surprising that accounts of Zuñi are often bewildering. In our own complex culture biography may be a clarifying form of description. Might it not avail at Zuñi? I venture this biography of Waiyautitsa.[30]

The biography which follows is the same as the *Scientific Monthly* essay, but her discussion of "men-women" and the feminist-edged rhetorical question with which she originally concluded are also deleted in the *American Indian Life* version. In their stead Parsons adds the following paragraph:

And yet among the Hopi, where the economy is practically identical with Zuñi, there are no men-women; in this tribe the institution, it is said, was never estab-slished. This, like other customs, is not merely a matter of economic adjustment; economics or psychologic propriety or consistency or predisposition may count, but of great importance also are the survival of traits from an earlier culture, and the acquiring of traits from the culture of neighboring peoples. Were we to understand the interplay of all these factors in the life, shall we say, of Waiyautitsa, we might be a long way towards understanding the principles of society, even other than that of Zuñi.[31]

Although admittedly a "fictional form of presentation" and influenced by a feminist bias, the discursive practices of this essay are not significantly different either from Parsons' "scientific" articles published in anthropological journals or the unpublished personal essays of "In the Southwest." Repeatedly, she uses biography as "a clarifying form of description," combines objective description with personal narrative and qualifies her "ethnographic authority" by making explicit her subject position, the circumstances of collecting and the limitations of her data. "The Zuñi La'mana," for example, begins as follows:

Of these 'men-women' there are today in Zuñi three or, one might almost say, three and a half—there is a boy about six years old qualifying, so to speak, for the status. An elderly Zuñi with whom I talked, a man over seventy, had known during his lifetime of nine *la'mana*. Mrs. Stevenson mentions five. Their names are Kasineli, Tsalatitse, and U'k. Kasineli I watched repeatedly in the audience of a five-day rain dance; Tsalatitse was pointed out to me in the street; U'k I failed to see or rather recognize during my first visit to Zuñi in August, he was taking part in the *ko'kokshi* when I began to look for him, in the last two of the five days' dance, and then I had to leave Zuñi. On my second visit in December, U'k was dancing again, but this time I saw him without a mask. The child, Laspeke (for Las Vegas), I had several opportunities to watch. Far from adequate, my observations may be nevertheless worth recording, so very little has been recorded at all about the Indian berdache. I hope to continue the study.[32]

Another example of the very different discursive space in which Parsons writes anthropology as well as the intimate relationships she established with Pueblo women is evident in the introduction to her essay "Mothers and Children at Laguna":

Wana's baby was two weeks old on my last (1918) visit to Laguna, and as the baby lay in her behooded board cradle on the floor or, still in her compartment, on the lap of her mother or her great-aunt, our talk led naturally from her and her short experience to ways with babies in general. Like other Pueblo Indian babies, she had been taken outdoors and presented to the gods. On the fourth morning of her life, before sunrise, one of the two surviving medicine-men of Laguna, the *shiwanna* (thunder) *cheani* came to the house and laid out on the floor of the upper room of the two-storied house his altar paraphernalia. Wana made for me the following diagram of the altar: On either side of the *iyetik* in our diagrammatic altar is a flint knife. The flint knives serve in this case, I surmise, as in other cases of ceremonial usage, as a guard to the *iyetik* or altar against witches or evil spirits . . . . Usually on altars the meal road leads from the east, the altar facing the east. I could not learn why in this instance the characteristic position was changed.[33]

If anything, Parsons' relationships with Hopi women were even more intimate, since she was adopted into a clan there, information with which she begins her essay on "Hopi Mothers and Children":

> My Sichumovi hostess—in Hopi terms 'my sister,' since after my head was washed I was regarded as of her clan—the Tansy Mustard (*asnyamo*) had had six girls, and she wanted a boy, so when she was pregnant again, at about the seventh month, she 'made a little boy,' to hang up in the back room where she kept her other ceremonial things. One of them, the stone fetich animal, the guardian that every Hopi house is possessed of and which is fed daily by the women of the house, I was never shown despite requests, but the doll baby (*tihu*) was promptly exhibited. To my surprise it was not the regular Hopi *tihu*, *kachina*-like, but, except for the somewhat mask-like face, an out-and-out American doll (*pahan tihu*), about two feet long, dressed in shirt and trousers. A more striking illustration of how the object of foreign material is ever fitted by Pueblo Indians into native pattern would be hard to find. For this American doll had performed the magical function of the kachina baby—my sister Anna had borne a boy after the pregnancy in question, and, the following year, another boy.[34]

In both these essays Parsons publishes "girl stuff" and "girl talk." It is doubtful that any male anthropologist could have or would have recorded the material in the essays in this volume—let alone published some of them in *Man*. He certainly would not have written about Hopi in this way, admitting the limitations of his knowledge of an/other way of life and accentuating the use of American dolls as kachina babies.

In the *Man* articles and the other essays reprinted here Parsons makes the conventional opening moves of modern ethnographic description that Mary Pratt has deftly analyzed. Presenting herself in the midst of the scenes and dialogue she relates, she anchors her description in "the intense and authority-giving personal experience of fieldwork."[35] Rather than assuming the authoritative ethnographic ground she has just cleared, however, Parsons explicitly undercuts it by admitting her ignorance and her limitations and by openly speculating. Her 1917 "Notes on Zuñi," for example, are quite literally that. In her more "mature" publications such as *Pueblo Indian Religion* (1939), she continues this practice in her footnotes and parenthetical asides, constructing a "mosaic" in both texts and footnotes—a polyphonic pastiche that mixes styles and genres,

*Elsie Clews Parsons
as she preferred to be,
in the Southwest at
San Gabriel Ranch,
Alcalde, New Mexico,
ca.1923. Photograph
courtesy of the
American Philo-
sophical Society.*

invoking, questioning and comparing the voices and authority of other anthropologists as well as her own previous inscriptions of Pueblo life. Not unlike Virginia Woolf, she interrupts, qualifies, and multiplies her own discourse—unwilling if not incapable of writing anthropology with monological masculine authority. As Parsons self-critically observed many years later in the American Anthropological Association presidential address that she did not live to deliver: "I am scrambling a good many things together that you would expect me to keep separate."[36]

The patchwork, quotative style that critics such as Melissa Meyer and Miriam Schapiro, Elaine Showalter, and Barbara Babcock have described as characteristic of women's expression and "the intercalation of mixed genres of texts and voices" that Paul Rabinow describes as "post-structuralist" ethnography is prefigured in Parsons' anthropological writing, which is indeed postmodern in its concern with how selves, cultures and discourses are constructed.[37] The subject position Parsons assumes and the "self" which she presents is "not a monolithic scientist-observer, but a multifaceted entity who participates, observes, and writes from multiple, constantly shifting positions."[38] But Parsons does not simply write multiply; she literally believes that anthropology should be a collaborative, cooperative enterprise. Rather than invisible informants behind the text, Margaret Lewis and others appear as authors themselves, and in more than one instance the Other has the last word or laugh, as in the conclusion to "The Zuñi La'mana":

> When prepared for burial the corpse of a *la'mana* is dressed in the usual woman's outfit, with one exception, under the woman's skirt a pair of trousers are put on. 'And on which side of the graveyard will he be buried?' I asked, with eagerness of heart if not of voice, for here at last was a test of the sex status of the *la'mana.* 'On the south side, the men's side, of course. *Kwash lu otse tea'me* (Is this man not)?' And my old friend smiled the peculiarly gentle smile he reserved for my particularly unintelligent questions.[39]

Parsons comments on the narrative presented in "Nativity Myth at Laguna and Zuñi" with a very interesting footnote describing the exchange between herself, the Zuni narrator Klippelanna and the translator who refuses to translate because he claims that the story is being told wrong and that if Parsons in turn told it wrong, then he would be held responsible.[40] In addition to sharing discursive space with her Pueblo collaborators, Parsons also shared significant periods of fieldwork with anthropologists A. L. Kroeber, Franz Boas, Esther S. Goldfrank and Ralph L. Beals and corresponded and shared materials with many others, notably Leslie A. White. Even when not literal co-authors, these other voices, Anglo and Indian, speak in the intertextuality of her prose.

The distinctiveness of Parsons' discourse and style of ethnographic authority in these essays on the Pueblo construction of gender is perhaps best seen when compared with descriptions of Pueblo motherhood by earlier and later anthropologists. Unlike Parsons, both Frank Hamilton Cushing, who preceded her at Zuni, and Dorothy Eggan, who followed her at Hopi, are interested in the institution of motherhood and the relations of reproduction in these "simpler" societies primarily for their contributions to what Cushing calls the "basis and center of every organization among men" and what Eggan terms "an adequate under-standing of the fundamentals involved in marital and family relations everywhere." There are also notable differences in style. Cushing, personal and patronizing, is the late nineteenth-century civilized man who lives among the "savages," returns to Washington to tell the National Congress of Mothers about "the little Zuñi mothers that I knew so well" and the savages who are "simply grown-up children . . . that I came to love . . . as I have loved no other children on earth." Eggan, writing in the 1950s, is "the writer" with questionnaires, impersonal and scientific.[41] Parsons, on the other hand, is able to write in the borderland between self and other without effacing or romanticizing either—in short, to write with irony.

Parsons' tone, her mixture of genres and her shifting and reflexive subject position confound those who would label her writing "popular" *or* "scholarly," "feminist" *or* "scientific."[42] Recognizing that "classification is nine-tenths of subjection" and associating certainty and conventionality with complacent masculinity, Parsons would most assuredly have object-ed to her biographers and critics' propensity to classify her as either a feminist *or* an anthropologist, to divide her research into before *and* after Boas, and to characterize her writing as either propaganda *or* science. Anthropologist and protege Leslie A. White, for example, asserts that "under [Boas' and Goddard's] influence, her intellectual posture shifted dramatically from the deductive sociology and weighty generalization of her early writings to a new concern for the smallest empirical detail of particular cultures." Most likely reading White rather than rereading Parsons, folklorist Richard Dorson similarly observed that "she shifted her allegiance from the sociology of Giddings to the anthropology of Franz Boas. . . . A long train of ethnological studies commencing in 1916 with Parson's first field reports on the Zuni show firmly the imprint of Boas, in the meticulous recording of cultural data, the sympathy to folklore, and the preference for empirical fact over speculative theory."[43]

Those familiar with Parsons' anthropology and who knew her better—Alfred Kroeber, Gladys Reichard and Ruth Bunzel for example— recognized a theoretical consistency throughout her career in her concern with the relationship between cultural forms and individual expression. She was, as Kroeber has remarked, grappling with the impact of culture on personality years before that problem was formally discovered by anthropologists and psychologists. In *The Golden Age of Anthropology*, Ruth Bunzel introduces Parsons as follows: "Externally, Elsie Clews Parsons' scientific life seems to fall into two distinct phases which might be called pre-Boas and post Boas. Actually, the distinction is more apparent than real. Throughout her life she consistently sought an answer to the problem of the nature of social pressures on the individual. It was only the techniques of her search that changed."[44] What both Kroeber and Bunzel do not say is that Parsons' primary concern was the relation between social formations and *female* subjectivity—in particular the cultural construction of gender and sexuality and reproduction, the sexual division of labor and the subjugation of women.

There were of course changes in the techniques of her search and in her discursive practices when Parsons turned from sociology to folklore and anthropology, but in the present essays the continuities seem far more important than the differences and the dichotomy between her feminism and her anthropology more apparent than real. "Could one," she asks in a March 1914 entry in "Journal of a Feminist," "get a more perfect bit of feminist propaganda by the ethnographic method?"[45] Whether consciously and ironically or not, this rhetorical question is an apt description of her own discursive practices after she began reading ethnology in 1905. After "raking through the ethnographic data" she would piece together a patchwork of customs from different cultures illustrating a particular idea. One of the most telling examples is the ironic assemblage of menstrual taboos for the "In Quarantine" chapter of *The Old Fashioned Woman: Primitive Fancies about the Sex:*

> But it is during menstruation that a woman is most generally considered dangerous. . . . The Bushmen think that at a glance from a menstruous women a man becomes at once transfixed and turned into a tree which talks. . . . The lips of any Omaha who ate with her would dry up and his blood turn black. . . . Under these circumstances quarantine is but a proper precaution. . . . A Sioux Indian agent tells me that once a month he had temporarily to release the Indian women prisoners, so great was the mens' objection to staying in prison with them at that time. . . . Besides seclusion all kinds of monthly taboos fall upon women. Thompson River woman may not make or mend a man's clothes or mocassins. . . . Aru Island women may not plant, cook, or prepare food. . . . as contagion is held

> to be very readily conveyed through food, food taboos fall upon menstruous women in many other places. The European peasant today believes that if a woman at this time enters a brewery the beer will turn sour. . . . In the great sugar refineries in the north of France, women are forbidden to enter the factory while the sugar is boiling or cooling, because the presence of a menstruous woman would blacken the sugar. Nor is any woman employed in opium manufacture at the French colony of Saigon lest, for the same reason, the opium should turn bitter.

Related examples include the pastiche of moral stories and supernatural sanctions used to police women that she assembles in "Links Between Religion and Morality in Early Culture," her first article published in the *American Anthropologist,* and her fascinating discussion (*a la* Mary Douglas) of the anomalousness and ceremonial segregation of widows in another 1915 article, "The Aversion to Anomalies," where in one short paragraph she gives examples from no less than six cultures.[46] As Leslie Spier remarked in his obituary essay, only keenness of insight and soundness of psychology saved Parsons from curiosity-shop speciousness. She was, nonetheless, guilty of what M. Z. Rosaldo has described as the feminist abuse of anthropology: using crosscultural data on women to comment on the position of women for better or worse in our own culture and to construct universal generalizations about women's status. "Primitive cultures," Parsons recalled years later, "were merely background for our own."[47]

Parsons' sociological perspective, however, was neither as evolutionary nor as universalizing as many of her critics and biographers have implied. Her early feminist sociology texts bear rereading not only for their challenge to the idea of cultural evolution and insistence on cultural relativism but also for her repeated questioning of "the social need for women's subordination."[48] There seems little doubt that the intent of her countless cross-cultural examples of the social construction of gender and sexuality is to document the degree to which "difference" is a matter of classification and control. From a post-modern anthropological perspective, Parsons' practice would seem less a matter of "abusing" anthropology for propaganda than of pioneering anthropology as a feminist cultural critique. Alfred Kroeber suggests this in his obituary essay: "Her choice of subject of study was almost certainly determined by the struggle of what she felt as self-preservation against family and environment. Her society had encroached on her; she studied the science of society the better to fight back against society."[49]

Apart from their readability and contribution to our understanding of Pueblo life, the essays collected in this volume are important as an early if invisible example of feminist anthropology. "Placing women at the center as subjects of inquiry and as active agents in the gathering of knowledge" while describing how gender, motherhood and reproduction are culturally constructed among the Pueblo,[50] Parsons anticipated contemporary feminist studies. She was perhaps the first to document and to demonstrate, as L. Drummond has much more recently, that

> far from being 'the most natural thing in the world' motherhood is in fact one of the most unnatural . . . rather than going on about the universal, biocultural innateness of something called a 'mother-child bond,' the process of conceiving, bearing and rearing a child should be viewed rather as a dilemma that strikes at the core of human understanding and evokes a heightened, not a diminished, cultural interpretation.[51]

In everything Elsie Clews Parsons wrote, but most obviously in these essays concerned with the Pueblo construction of "the most natural thing in the world," she challenged the naturalizing and essentializing which is the basis of racist and sexist ideologies. As Franz Boas recognized, it was this "critical attitude" and "courageous expression" that made her "a power for good in our society."[52]

NOTES

1. Boas (1942a:480). The portions of this essay concerning the relationship between Parsons' feminism and her anthropology, challenging the before-and-after-Boas characterization of Parsons' professional life and examining her discursive practices, were originally written and presented as a paper (Babcock 1988).

2. For more on the relationship between Parsons' feminist writings and the reemergence of feminism in anthropology in the 1970s and 1980s, see Lamphere (1989). For contemporary feminist discussions of motherhood et al, see Chodorow (1978), Drummond (1978), Garner et al (1985), Grosz (1989), Kristeva (1980,1985), Martin (1987), Moore (1988), O'Brien (1981), Paige and Paige (1981), Rich (1976), Stanton (1986), Trebilcot (1984), Van Buren (1989) and Weigle (1989).

3. Kroeber to Parsons, 1/13/16. Letters referenced in this manner refer to correspondence in the Elsie Clews Parsons papers in the American Philosophical Society Library, Philadelphia, Pennsylvania, and are cited with its permission. Parsons to Lowie quoted in Hare (1985:135-39).

4. I once suggested wrongly that Parsons for twenty-two years after her letter to Lowie did "folklore and anthropological scholarship [that] may be characterized as an atheoretical compendium of empirical fact with both theory and personal observations relegated to the footnotes, in contrast to the speculative theory and personal style of her feminist sociology" (Babcock 1987:397).

5. Among Parsons' papers at the American Philosophical Society is an index card file of all essays she submitted for publication between 1914 and 1921. For each entry there is a "date" and a "fate" column. The patterns of rejection recorded thus as well as correspondence concerning her publications are compelling evidence of how necessary it is, as Mulcahy (1984) has suggested, following Foucault, to view Parsons' work as part of a "discursive formation"—in relation to the larger cultural arena which influenced her thinking and to which she actively contributed.

6. Quoted in Hare (1985:138).

7. Quoted in Hare (1985:126).

8. James Clifford makes this point about the ironic stance of participant observation and the nature of ethnographic knowledge in several important essays, notably "On Ethnographic Authority" (1983) and "On Ethnographic Self-Fashioning"(1988).

9. Parsons (n.d.c).

10. Quoted in Rosenberg (1982:168).

11. Parsons (1906:198). Parsons' relations with Native American women and her writing about them stand in striking contrast to the "matronizing" behavior and discourse of the majority of Anglo women social workers and anthropologists. Unlike such predecessors and successors in the Southwest as Matilda Coxe Stevenson, Gladys Reichard and Alice Marriott, Parsons seems critically and ironically self-aware of the colonial situation of the anthropologist and the complexity of educating herself as well as her society. For discussion of Linda Gordon's concept of "matronization," the dynamics of matronization in the relations of Anglo and Indian women, and maternal authority in the stories anthropologists told about indigenous southwestern women, see D. Gordon (1986). Obviously I disagree here and elsewhere in this essay with those who have argued—most recently Lamphere (1989)—that Parsons did not bring her feminism to her anthropology.

12. Kroeber to Parsons, 8/10/15; Parsons to H. Parsons, 8/15/15.

13. Although at one time she clearly intended to publish these very personal and accessible accounts of her early Southwest field experiences, Parsons never did. I am presently editing this collection for publication with the University of New Mexico Press.

14. Lamphere (1989).

15. For discussion of Luce Irigaray's position on the relation between maternity and feminism which Parsons anticipates and which stands in marked contrast to, e.g., Simone de Beauvoir, see Grosz (1989:120). For a critique of the use of the maternal metaphor in the theorizing of contemporary French feminists, see Stanton (1986).

16. Grosz (1989:78, 81).

17. Moore (1988:25), who further discusses recent feminist critiques in anthropology. In the forward to *Of Woman Born* Adrienne Rich (1976:15) remarks: "I wanted to write a book on motherhood because it was a crucial, still relatively unexplored, area for feminist theory." Unfortunately, Rich, like other contemporary feminists, is unaware of Parsons' contributions to this subject.

18. Haeberlin (1916:28). See Black (1984), Young (1987) and Babcock (1989) for recent discussion of the symbolics of reproduction in Pueblo culture. In addition to examining the significance of the "idea of fertilization" in Pueblo life, Babcock is also concerned with the politics of the reproduction of the reproduction of culture in such cultural forms as stories and potteries.

19. Moore (1988:25).

20. Cushing (1897); Haeberlin (1916).

21. Moore (1988:37); Collier and Rosaldo (1981); Malinowski (1962:62). Not surprisingly, since they worked at Zuni together and shared ideas, Parsons' treatment of kinship reflected Kroeber's emphasis on language and psychology. For further discussion of Kroeber's "Zuñi Kin and Clan" (1917), its importance and its influence on American kinship studies, see Hoebel (1954:721-22).

22. Parsons (1937:109).

23. Parsons (1939b:338, 340).

24. Parsons (1919d:457).

25. Kluckhohn (1954:685).

26. Parsons (1922:1); Spier (1943:248-49).

27. Moore (1988:38).

28. Parsons (1919d:443).

29. For further discussion of the "approach" and the initial view of the Other characteristic of turn-of-the-century travel narrative and carried into the opening moves of ethnographies, see Pratt (1986a, 1986b) and Hinsley (1991). In the latter essay, "Authoring Authenticity," which deals specifically with the imaging of Southwestern landscapes in popular and anthropological literature between 1875 and 1915, Hinsley focuses on Cushing's approach to Zuni—an approach that Parsons repeats here "with a difference."

30. Parsons (1922:157-58).

31. Ibid:172-73.

32. Parsons (1916b:521).

33. Parsons (1919b:34-35).

34. Parsons (1921a:98).

35. Pratt (1986b:32).

36. Parsons (1942:339).

37. Meyer and Schapiro (1978); Showalter (1986); Babcock (1987); Rabinow (1983). For further discussion of these issues in ethnographic discourse, see Clifford (1983, 1988); Clifford and Marcus (1986). See Mulcahy (1984:11) for more on the relationship of Parsons' "mosaic" style to Boas's preoccupation with cultural "elements" and "wholes." Lamphere also describes Parsons as writing in "a polyphonic Boasian mode"(1989:523). I should point out, however, that these sections of my essay concerning Parsons' discursive practices were largely written over two years ago (see Babcock 1988) and are in no way derived from Lamphere.

38. Pratt (1986b:39).

39. Parsons (1916b:528).

40. Parsons (1918b:258, fn.5). For further discussion of heteroglossia and plural authorship, see Clifford (1983:139-40).

41. Cushing (1897:21, 24); Eggan (1944:6).
42. See Mulcahy (1984:19) for interesting speculation on disciplinary chauvinism and attempts to classify Parsons and her writing.
43. Parsons (1916a:55); White (1973:582); Dorson (1974:23-24). Regrettably, Dorson also claims that "her unconventional field sorties finally led to a rigid and colorless scholarship, as if she were determined to prove the masculinity of her mind by removing all sentiment or even humanity from her ethnology." I cannot but wonder what of Parsons' Pueblo ethnology Dorson actually did read. Certainly not the essays collected in this volume.
44. Kroeber (1943:254); Reichard (1943); Bunzel (1960:546). Kroeber, Bunzel and Kluckhohn (1954) assert that Parsons was a pioneer in both theorizing and documenting the relationship between culture and the individual and that much of her Pueblo ethnography was indeed concerned with culture and personality issues. Lamphere (1989) argues to the contrary.
45. Parsons (n.d.b).
46. Parsons (1913a:91-97; 1915a; 1915b).
47. Spier (1943:246); Rosaldo (1980); Parsons (n.d.d).
48. Rosenberg (1982:147).
49. Kroeber (1943:252).
50. Strathern (1987:277).
51. Drummond (1978:31).
52. Boas (1942a:480; 1942b:90).

References Cited

Babcock, Barbara A.
 1987 Taking Liberties, Writing from the Margins, and Doing It with a
     Difference. *Journal of American Folklore* 100(398):390-411.
 1988 'Not Yet Classified, Perhaps Not Classifiable':Elsie Clews Parsons,
     Feminist/Anthropologist. Paper presented at the American
     Anthropological Association Meetings, November 16.
 1989 'At Home, No Womens are Storytellers': Potteries, Stories, and Politics
     in Cochiti Pueblo. *Journal of the Southwest* 30(3):356-389.
Benedict, Ruth F.
 1940 Women and Anthropology. In *The Education of Women in a
     Democracy*, edited and published by The Institute of Professional
     Relations for The Women's Centennial Congress, New York.
Black, Mary E.
 1984 Maidens and Metaphors: An Analysis of Hopi Corn
     Metaphors. *Ethnology* 23(4):279-288.
Boas, Franz
 1942a Elsie Clews Parsons. *Scientific Monthly* 54:480-482.
 1942b Elsie Clews Parsons. *Science* 95(2456):89-90.
Bunzel, Ruth L.
 1960 Elsie Clews Parsons, 1975-1941. In Margaret Mead and Ruth Bunzel,
     eds. *The Golden Age of American Anthropology*. New York:George
     Braziller. Pp. 546-547.
Chodorow, Nancy
 1978 *The Reproduction of Mothering: Psychoanalysis and the Sociology of
     Gender*. Berkeley: University of California Press.
Clifford, James
 1983 On Ethnographic Authority. *Representations* 2:118-146.
 1988 *The Predicament of Culture:Twentieth-Century Ethnography,
     Literature, and Art*. Cambridge:Harvard University Press.
Clifford, James and Marcus, George E., eds.
 1986 *Writing Culture:The Politics and Poetics of Ethnography*. Berkeley:
     University of California Press.
Collier, Jane F. and Michelle Z. Rosaldo
 1981 Politics and gender in simple societies. In Sherry B. Ortner and
     Harriet Whitehead, eds. *Sexual Meanings:The Cultural Construction
     of Gender and Sexuality*. Cambridge:Cambridge University Press.
     Pp. 275-329.
Cushing, Frank Hamilton
 1897 Primitive Motherhood. *The Work and Words of the National Congress
     of Mothers*. New York:D. Appleton and Company. Pp. 21-47.
Dorson, Richard M.
 1974 Elsie Clews Parsons:Feminist and Folklorist. *Folklore Feminists
     Communication* 2(4):22-25.
Drummond, L.
 1978 The transatlantic nanny:notes on a comparative semiotics of the
     family in English-speaking societies. *American Ethnologist*
     5(1):30-43.
Eggan, Dorothy
 1944 Hopi Marriage and Family Relations. *Marriage and Family Living*
     6:1, 2, 6.

Garner, Shirley Nelson, Claire Kahane, and Madelon Sprengnether, eds.
1985   *The (M)other Tongue:Essays in Feminist Psychoanalytic
            Interpretation*. Ithaca:Cornell University Press.
Gordon, Deborah
1986   Among Women:Gender and Ethnographic Authority in the
            Southwest, 1930-1980. Paper prepared for the Daughters of the
            Desert Symposium, Wenner-Gren Foundation. March 12-23,
            Tucson, AZ.
Grosz, Elizabeth
1989   *Sexual Subversions:Three French Feminists*. Sydney:Allen & Unwin.
Haeberlin, H. K.
1916   The Idea of Fertilization in the Culture of the Pueblo Indians.
            Memoirs of the American Anthropological Association 3(13-16):1-55.
Hare, Peter H.
1985   *A Woman's Quest for Science:Portrait of Anthropologist Elsie Clews
            Parsons*. Buffalo:Prometheus Books.
Hinsley, Curtis M., Jr.
1991   Authoring Authenticity. In Barbara A. Babcock and
            Joseph Wilder, eds. *Inventing the Southwest:Region as
            Commodity*. Special issue of *Journal of the Southwest*. Forthcoming.
Hoebel, E. Adamson
1954   Major Contributions of Southwestern Studies to Anthropological
            Theory. *American Anthropologist* 56(4):720-727.
Kluckhohn, Clyde
1954   Southwestern Studies of Culture and Personality. *American
            Anthropologist* 56(4):685-708.
Kristeva, Julia
1980   *Desire in Language:A Semiotic Approach to Literature and Art*.
            New York:Columbia University Press.
1985   Stabat Mater. *Poetics Today* 6(1-2):133-152.
Kroeber, Alfred L.
1917   Zuñi Kin and Clan. *Anthropological Papers of the American Museum
            of Natural History* Vol. 18, Pt. 2.
1943   Elsie Clews Parsons. *American Anthropologist* 45:252- 255.
Lamphere, Louise
1989   Feminist Anthropology:The Legacy of Elsie Clews Parsons.
            American Ethnologist 16(3):518-533.
Malinowski, Bronislaw
1962   Parenthood—The Basis of Social Structure (1930). In *Sex, Culture,
            and Myth*. New York:Harcourt, Brace & World. Pp. 42-88.
Martin, Emily
1987   *The Woman in the Body:A Cultural Analysis of Reproduction*.
            Boston:Beacon Press.
Meyer, Melissa and Miriam Schapiro
1978   Waste Not, Want Not. *Heresies* 4:66-69.
Moore, Henrietta L.
1988   *Feminism and Anthropology*. Minneapolis:University of
            Minnesota Press.
Mulcahy, Joanne B.
1984   Elsie Clews Parsons and Folklore Theory: A Productive Marginality.
            Unpublished MS.
O'Brien, Mary
1981   *The Politics of Reproduction*. Boston:Routledge & Kegan Paul.

Ortner, Sherry B. and Harriet Whitehead,eds.
    1981   *Sexual Meanings:The Cultural Construction of Gender and Sexuality.*
            Cambridge:Cambridge University Press.

Paige, Karen Ericksen and Jeffery M. Paige
    1981   *The Politics of Reproductive Ritual.* Berkeley:University of
            California Press.

Parsons, Elsie Clews
    n.d.a   Correspondence. Unpublished papers, American Philosophical
            Society.
    n.d.b   Journal of a Feminist. Unpublished manuscript, American
            Philosophical Society.
    n.d.c   In the Southwest. Unpublished manuscript, American Philosopical
            Society. [Being edited for publication by Barbara A. Babcock.
            Forthcoming, University of New Mexico Press]
    n.d.d   The World Changes. Unpublished fragment, American
            Philosophical Society.
    1906   *The Family.* New York:G.P. Putnam's Sons.
    1913   *The Old-Fashioned Woman:Primitive Fancies About the Sex.* New
            York:G. P. Putnam's Sons.
    1915a   Links between Religion and Morality in Early Culture. *American
            Anthropologist* 17:41-57.
    1915b   The Aversion to Anomalies. *The Journal of Philosophy* 12:212-219.
    1915c   Zuñi Conception and Pregnancy Beliefs. *Proceedings of the 19th
            International Congress of Americanists.* Pp. 379-383.
    1916a   *Social Rule.* New York:G.P. Putnam's Sons.
    1916b   The Zuñi La'mana. *American Anthropologist* 18:521-528.
    1917   Notes on Zuñi, Pts. I & II. *American Anthropological Association
            Memoir,* No. 4.
    1918a   Review of *Zuñi Kin and Clan* by A.L. Kroeber. *American
            Anthropologist* 20:98-104.
    1918b   Nativity Myth at Laguna and Zuñi. *Journal of American Folklore*
            31:256-63.
    1919a   Increase by Magic:A Zuñi Pattern. *American Anthropologist*
            21:279-86.
    1919b   Mothers and Children at Laguna. *Man* 17-18:34-38
    1919c   Mothers and Children at Zuñi, New Mexico. *Man* 19:168-173.
    1919d   Waiyautitsa of Zuñi, New Mexico. *Scientific Monthly* 9:443-457.
            (Reprinted in Parsons 1922).
    1921a   Hopi Mothers and Children. *Man* 57-58:98-104.
    1921b   Getting Married on First Mesa, Arizona. *The Scientific Monthly*
            13:259-265.
    1922   *American Indian Life.* New York:B. W. Huebsch.
    1923   *Laguna Genealogies* (Anthropological Papers American Museum
            Natural History 19:133-292).
    1924   Tewa Mothers and Children. *Man* 112:148-151.
    1926   *Tewa Tales* (Memoirs of the American Folklore Society 19).
    1929   *The Social Organization of the Tewa in New Mexico* (Memoirs
            American Anthropological Association 36).
    1936   *Taos Pueblo* (General Series in Anthropology 2).
    1937   Review of *Zuñi Mythology* by Ruth Benedict and *Zuñi Texts* by Ruth
            Bunzel. *Journal of American Folklore* 50:107-109.
    1939a   *Pueblo Indian Religion,* 2 vols. Chicago:University of Chicago Press.
    1939b   The Last Zuñi Transvestite. *American Anthropologist* 41:338-340.
    1942   Anthropology and Prediction. *American Anthropologist*
            44(3):337-344.

Pratt, Mary Louise
    1986a   Scratches on the Face of the Country; or, What Mr. Barrow Saw in the Land of the Bushmen. In Henry Louis Gates, Jr., *"Race," Writing, and Difference*. Chicago:University of Chicago Press. Pp. 138-162.
    1986b   Fieldwork in Common Places. In James Clifford and George E. Marcus, eds. *Writing Culture:The Poetics and Politics of Ethnography*. Berkeley:University of California Press. Pp. 27-50.

Rabinow, Paul
    1983   "Facts are a word of God":An Essay Review of James Clifford's *Person and Myth: Maurice Leenhardt in the Melanesian World*. In George W. Stocking, Jr., ed. *Observers Observed:Essays on Ethnographic Fieldwork. History of Anthropology*, Vol. I. Madison: The University of Wisconsin Press. Pp. 196-207.

Reichard, Gladys
    1943   Elsie Clews Parsons. *Journal of American Folklore* 56:45-48.

Rich, Adrienne
    1976   *Of Woman Born:Motherhood as Experience and Institution*. New York:W.W. Norton & Company.

Rosaldo, M. Z.
    1980   The Use and Abuse of Anthropology:Reflections on Feminism and Cross-cultural Understanding. *Signs* 5(3):389-417.

Rosenberg, Rosalind
    1982   *Beyond Separate Spheres:Intellectual Roots of Modern Feminism*. New Haven:Yale University Press.

Showalter, Elaine
    1986   Piecing and Writing. In Nancy K. Miller, ed. *The Poetics of Gender*. New York:Columbia University Press. Pp. 222-247.

Spier, Leslie
    1943   Elsie Clews Parsons. *American Anthropologist* 45:244-251.

Stanton, Domna C.
    1986   Difference on Trial: A Critique of the Maternal   Metaphor in Cixous, Irigaray, and Kristeva. In Nancy K. Miller, ed. *A Poetics of Gender*. New York:Columbia University Press. Pp. 157-182.

Strathern, Marilyn
    1987   An Awkward Relationship:The Case of Feminism and Anthropology. *Signs* 12 (2):276-292.

Trebilcot, Joyce, ed.
    1984   *Mothering:Essays in Feminist Theory*. Totowa, N.J.:Rowman and Allanheld Publishers.

Van Buren, Jane Silverman
    1989   *The Modernist Madonna:Semiotics of the Maternal Metaphor*. Bloomington:Indiana University Press.

Weigle, Marta
    1989   *Creation and Procreation:Feminist Reflections on Cosmogony and Parturition*. Philadelphia:University of Pennsylvania Press.

White, Leslie
    1973   Elsie Clews Parsons. In Edward T. James, ed. *Dictionary of American Biography*, Supplement 3 (1941-45). New York:Charles Scribner's Sons. Pp. 581-2.

Young, M. Jane
    1987   Women, Reproduction, and Religion in Western Puebloan Society. *Journal of American Folklore* 100(398):435-445.

Zuñi Conception and Pregnancy Beliefs

There are two shrines near Zuñi to which would-be or expectant mothers resort, women whose children have died and who wish for another child, or women who wish to determine the sex of their unborn child. The more popular shrine of the two is near the base of the towering and semi-detached rock which rises into sharp pinnacles on the northwestern side of To'wa Ya'lene, Corn mountain, the impressive mesa about three miles to the east of the pueblo. Part of *a'giapa'* (*a*, plural prefix; *giapa*, wide), as the Zuñi call this pinnacled rock,[1] makes a picture, from a certain angle, of a woman with a child on her back.[2] In one creation story *a'giapa'* represents the five children born to the sacrificed son and daughter of the rain priests, the couple sacrificed at the time of the great flood. At the base of *a'giapa'*, cut on the face of an overhung shelf there is a quantity of phallic symbols,[3] particularly the *a'sha* or vulva, and along the western trail to the top of the mesa these symbols are scattered. One of them, an *a'sha* three or four times life size, is particularly noticeable about two and a half feet above the trail where steps have been notched into a somewhat precipitous white sandstone slope. Removed from any of these conspicuous symbols, however, is the shrine itself. It lies to the south of the most symbol-covered rock and above it—quite off the trail. Here in a steep turn of *a'giapa'* stands a much weathered post, about six by four inches and two and a half feet high. Near its top is a rudely cut face. About two feet in the slope above the little upright stretches east and west a straight line of prayer-plumes. I counted more than two dozen of them set contiguous to one another. All were of the same height, less than a foot. Other prayer-plumes lay in the soil near by, as if washed from their setting. The plume-stick representing a prayer for a boy has a bit of turquoise paint under the face cut in it. The face is surmounted by a bit of terracing. The plume-stick for the girl is topped off flatly in the same form as the wooden upright. These *te'likinawe* have been made for the prayerful woman by a *shiwani*, or rain priest, and he it is who accompanies her to the shrine.[5]

The other phallic shrine is an open loop of stones set as a wall about three feet high standing on the edge of a road which happens to lead to some cornfields. The spot is about a third of a mile northwest of To'wa Ya'lene. The loop opens to the east. Opposite, a half-buried stone projects inward about a foot and a half. From this stone a bit is chipped off by the

Facing Page:

Zuni Mother and child, ca. 1908. Photograph by H.F. Robinson. Courtesy of the Museum of New Mexico, Negative no. 37341.

husband or kinsman of the pregnant woman who is wishful of a daughter. A few weeks before her confinement she drinks a potion containing the powdered bit of stone.[6] It is not customary to plant plumes near this shrine.[7]

There is also a plant decoction which the would-be mother of a girl will drink.[8] Moreover to insure the birth of a girl the men must be sent out of the house during the labor.[9] The year-old child of my hostess in Zuñi, a Cherokee married to a Zuñi, is a boy. His mother had wanted a girl. "You should not have had in the American doctor[10] then," her Zuñi friends had in substance said to her, "nor should the father have been present."

In connection with both rabbit and deer hunting there are conception beliefs. After the quadrennial rabbit hunt in which the *Ko'ko*, or sacred personages, take part, the *Cha'kwena*, the Rabbit Huntress or Mother, retires to the *he'kiapa ke'witsine* or kiva,[11] and lies-in on the regulation maternity sand bed. Here the would-be mother looks after her. An ear of mother corn represents the infant. The *Cha'kwena* may not leave the *ke'witsine*, but the would-be mother is not so strictly confined. At the close of four days[12] the would-be mother bathes the *Cha'kwena* and gives her a *ja'tonane*, a regulation woman's dress, and a pair of woman's moccasins. The two ears of corn that have been worn in the rabbit hunt by the *Cha'kwena* are taken home by the would-be mother and worn one day in her own belt. She has given two other ears of corn to the *Cha'kwena*. It is the blood mother of the *Cha'kwena* (the mask is personated by a man) who attends the would-be mother when in due course she is confined, and the man representing the *Cha'kwena* therefore[13] becomes the ceremonial father of the child at his initiation into the *ko'tikili*.[14]

In this connection a generalized phallic rite performed by the *Cha'kwena* as part of the rabbit hunt should be mentioned. Four days before the hunt a rabbit is killed and its blood is smeared on the legs of the *Cha'kwena*.[15] During the hunt it is obligatory on the *Cha'kwena* to go in a straight line, no matter what growths she must pass through, in order that the blood that has been smeared on her legs may be rubbed off on the plants in her route, thereby causing the rabbits to be plentiful. Likewise the human infants of Zuñi. If the hunt is not conducted strictly, if the *Cha'kwena* is not properly stage-managed, so to speak, there will be few rabbits and few children. The association between rabbits and infants is obvious enough, but I was definitely told that rabbits are thought of in connection with child-bearing because they are prolific, and their young vigorous—one of the endless instances of the use of imitative magic or of the habit of analogous thinking at Zuñi.

The conception belief in connection with deer is another instance. Because deer have twins, if a woman unwittingly eats[16] the wafer bread

The "phallic shrine" at the base of a'giapa', "The Mother Rock," a semi-detached rock on the northwestern side of To'wa Ya'lene, Corn Mountain, where expectant mothers go, ca. 1886. Photograph by I.W. Taber. Courtesy of the Museum of New Mexico, Negative no. 89948.

her husband has taken with him on a deer hunt and has brought back home, she too will be delivered of twins. If she wants to eat the bread with impunity it must be passed four times round the rung of her house ladder. The woman who eats at the same meal venison and mutton or venison and beef, will also become, it is believed, the mother of twins.[17]

During pregnancy there are several restrictions upon one or the other of the expectant parents. A pregnant woman should not take part in dyeing wool or even look on; it would spoil the color. Nor should she fire pottery; it would bring out black spots in the ware.[18] In these cases and others I shall give it is difficult to be sure how strictly the taboo is followed. I got the impression that if the color were spoiled or black spots appeared it was merely put down to the presence of a pregnant woman. Another pregnancy taboo, the taboo against looking on a corpse, is undoubtedly more heeded, in this case no chances being taken. The child would be still-born or, born alive, it would soon pine away.

There are rules to facilitate labor. A woman is told not to eat piñon nuts, for it would increase the "grease" on the child's head and so delay delivery. She is told too not to stand at windows. Like its mother, the unborn child will stay still in the womb before the outlet into another place.[19] To hasten labor a bean may be swallowed by the anxious woman—the growth of the bean is very quick.[20]

A pregnant woman should not scatter bran on her oven floor—a method of testing temperature—otherwise her child will have pimples.[21] Albinism is caused by a parent-to-be eating the white leaf inside the corn-husk; by the husband eating it before the conception or by the wife eating it afterward. In the case of the albino I asked questions about, it was her father, I was told, who had been responsible.[22] During the pregnancy a husband must be very circumspect in his treatment of animals. Were he to shoot a rabbit or a prairie-dog the child would be marked or deformed in a way corresponding to the injury suffered by the animal—blind or lame or malformed. The head of one little girl I knew was a bit flattened on one side. It was so, they said, because before her birth her father shot prairie-dogs in the head. The same man had been himself marked at birth on his forehead and chest with a raised mark like the entrail of an animal due to his father having danced in a ceremony in which entrails were slung around the body —the father was a member of the Ne'wekwe, or Galaxy fraternity, a fraternity characterized by this practice.[23] Another man I knew had a deformed jaw. It was probably due, they said, to his father or mother[24] having broken during the pregnancy the jaws of a sheep. Of any killing of animals the most fatal to the unborn child[25] is the killing of a snake. The child will be born spotted like a snake and will die.

To get rid of the birth-mark or deformity, the method, we may say, is one of inoculation. The animal that has been the source of the trouble

Zuni children, ca. 1920. Courtesy of the Museum of New Mexico, Negative no. 145951.

should be killed and its blood rubbed on the suffering child. Again, if an infant cries much the chance is that its back was hurt because its father maltreated some horses before its birth. To cure it, its father should drive a team hard and then rub the sweat from under their collars or harness on the child's back. Similarly, to cure the mark due to the father taking part in a dance during the pregnancy, the dance mask should be put on, the father should dance hard in the presence of the child, and should then rub his sweat on the child. Deafness in a child[26] is supposed to be due to stealing by its mother before its birth. To cure it, its mother should steal something, burn the object stolen, and put the ashes in the child's ears.

Notes

Originally published in F. W. Hodge, ed., *Proceedings of the Nineteenth International Congress of Americanists*, Held at Washington, D.C., December 27-31, 1915 (Washington, D.C., 1917), pp. 379-383. The original footnotes have been renumbered consecutively as endnotes.

1. "The Mother Rock," Mrs Stevenson has called it..
2. This outline, to the Zuñi woman who called my attention to it, seemed reason enough for the position of the phallic shrine.
3. An excellent picture of them is given by Mrs Stevenson, "The Zuñi Indians," pl. XII, *Twenty-third Ann. Rep. Bur. Amer. Ethnol.* (1901-02).
4. To the Zuñi the turquoise is male.
5. Not, according to Mrs Stevenson, her husband or kinswoman or a medicine-woman. ("The Zuñi Indians," p. 294.) The point is perhaps important—to one inclined to draw inferences from analogy with phallic practices elsewhere.

   Mrs Stevenson states that prayer-plumes are planted only for a boy. For a girl the rock is scraped, she says, and deposited in a tiny, specially made vase in a cavity in the rock. I failed to examine these honeycomb cavities. Dr Fewkes found in them only bits of woolen thread. ("A Few Summer Ceremonials at Zuñi Pueblo," *Journ. Amer. Ethnology and Archæology*, 1891, I, 9-10.) The shrine itself he failed to see.

   Since my visit to To'wa Ya'lene I have tried to verify Mrs Stevenson's statements about the deposits in the rock cavities, but I have failed. The custom of depositing a bit of thread in a cavity is not a pregnancy custom. The thread was taken from the belt and the practice is or was, I believe, a love charm.
6. A not altogether reliable Zuñi woman told me that the clay brought from To'wa Ya'lene to make pottery—*gawinakate kune*, water-jar clay—is powdered and drunk for the same purpose.
7. Unfortunately I failed to examine the chipped stone to see if the chipping were recent, but I was told that the shrine was little resorted to. Several of its stones, I noticed, were tumbled down.

   Mrs Stevenson describes a third shrine, a stone shrine for the getting of sons; but I have failed to obtain any mention of it.

   The wearing of shells in the belt to determine sex, a custom Mrs Stevenson describes ("The Zuñi Indians," p. 296), is not a Zuñi custom. It may be Navaho, my Zuñi informants suggested.
8. M. C. Stevenson, "Ethnobotany of the Zuñi Indians," p. 84, *Thirtieth Ann. Rep. Bur. Amer. Ethnol.* (1908-09), 1915.
9. They are sent out, at any rate, although it is more than likely that in some cases at least a boy is wished for. One gets the impression that at Zuñi girls are the preferred offspring. One of the reasons *alleged* for the making of a *la'mana*, the "man-woman" of the Zuñi, is a shortage of girls to do the women's work in the household.
10. For this reason, if not for other Zuñi points of view, the male physician who has been on the reservation for twelve years has no obstetrical cases among the Zuñi.
11. It lies on the west side of the pueblo. It is the *ke'witse* of the nadir.
12. The customary confinement period differs in different families:it may be four days or eight or ten or twelve. But whatever the family custom, were it not followed, the woman, it is believed, would "dry up," get thin and die. Among the Hopi the period is four days (J. G. Owens, "Natal Ceremonies of the Hopi Indians," *Jour. Amer. Ethnol. and Archæol.*, II, 1892, p. 166).

13. The regular Zuñi custom is for the husband of the woman who first touches the child at his delivery to become his ceremonial father.

14. Cf. Mrs Stevenson's account of this phallic rite ("The Zuñi Indians," p. 93). Her statements that the *Cha'kwena* gives *te'likinawe* to would-be mothers and that in her progress through the pueblo pregnant women made a point of gazing upon her (pp. 90, 140), I was unable to verify.

15. Mrs Stevenson's version differs. She states that in the hunt "the first rabbit killed has its nose cut and is handed to the *Cha'kwena* by a maiden, and the *Cha'kwena* rubs the bleeding nose down her legs on the inner sides, that the A'shiwi (Zuñi) girls may hasten to arrive at the age of puberty and that they may be prolific in child-bearing." ("The Zuñi Indians," p. 92.)

    This account sounds to me like the now obsolete practice at Santa Clara. That Mrs Stevenson once took part in a Santa Clara rabbit hunt is a well remembered fact, because, thanks to her unwelcomed attendance, the hunt had to be made over again.

    The *Cha'kwena* must belong to the Badger clan, as Mrs. Stevenson points out, or (as she fails to point out), he may be a child of the Badger clan, i.e. his father may be a Badger. The two brothers who now play the part belong to the Eagle clan. They learned the part from their father, i.e. their blood father.

16. Only unwittingly would she eat this particular portion of bread, because it has been made "sacred" to the deer and to the dead.

17. In the tales recorded by Cushing the description of twins as being as like each to each as "two deer born of the same mother" is common. See Zuñi Folk Tales, pp. 307, 469, New York, 1901. Are there other instances elsewhere, I would like to ask, of the concomitance of stereotype similes and practices of sympathetic magic?

18. Noted too in "The Zuñi Indians," p. 377.

19. Because the *piwani*, or weasel, gets out easily through a hole, its meat is given to a Hopi woman to facilitate parturition. (Dorsey and Voth, "The Oraibi Soyal Ceremony," *Field Columbian Museum Pub. 55. Anthrop. Ser.*, vol. III, no. 1, p. 34 note; Owens, op. cit., p. 165.) This practice is unknown at Zuñi.

20. This practice was denied by my more reliable authorities; nevertheless, given certain circumstances under which the information was imparted, I am inclined to credit it.

21. Here again and in all of the following cases the amount of fidelity to the taboo is hard to gauge. But if offspring have the peculiarity in question it is certainly accounted for by some act of parental carelessness.

22. The Pueblo story goes that she was the second albino in her family and that her mother was so ashamed of her that she once tried to burn her to death. My informant believed that parents generally would be ashamed of albino offspring. There appears to be no prejudice at large however against albinos. Cf. too Hrdlicka, "Physiological and Medical Observations among the Indians of Southwestern United States and Northern Mexico," *Bull. 34, Bur. Amer. Ethnol.*, 1908, p. 194. But Hrdlicka notes too that the albinos are ashamed of their condition, bashful, sensitive. Parental prejudice would obviously be a factor in such self-consciousness.

    There are three albinos today in Zuñi—one woman, two children.

23. It was the father himself who was my informant.

24. A greater number of pregnancy taboos fall upon the father, I was expressly told, than upon the mother. These taboos were noted in general terms by Cushing, but he read into them, I am inclined to believe, our own theory of prenatal maternal impressions. "What the mother looked most on while withholding them," Cushing records in a creation myth of the *ko'yemshi*, "thuswise were they formed as clay by the thought of the potter; wherefore we cherish our matrons and reveal not to them the evil dramas, neither the slaughtered nor hamstrung game lest their children be weakly or go maimed." Again, "their anxieties are like to press themselves on the unripe and forming children in their bowels. Wherefore also we guard our eyes from all weird seeming things when they be with child." ("Zuñi Creation Myths," *Thirteenth Ann. Rep. Bur.*

Amer. Ethnol. (1891-92), pp. 401, 406.) More specifically Cushing reports that pregnant women must be guarded "from the sight of moving water, fish, and water reptiles no less than from fierce and fearful things." (*J. Amer. Folk-Lore*, 1898, IX, p. 110.) The taboo on viewing moving water and water creatures I have been unable to verify.

25. At no time for his children's sake, should a man kill a snake.
26. Not at birth, but in later childhood. No case of deafness at birth was known to my elderly informant.

We-wha, the Zuni transvestite who worked with Matilda Coxe Stevenson, in ceremonial dress, weaving a belt at the Smithsonian Institution, Washington, D.C., ca. 1888. Courtesy of the Museum of New Mexico, Negative no. 2565.

The Zuñi La'mana

Of these "men-women" there are today in Zuñi three or, one might almost say, three and a half—there is a boy about six years old qualifying, so to speak, for the status. An elderly Zuñi with whom I talked, a man over seventy, had known during his lifetime of nine *la'mana*. Mrs. Stevenson mentions five.[1] The three adults now living are about the same age, in the late thirties and early forties. Their names are Kasineli, Tsalatitse, and U'k.[2] Kasineli I watched repeatedly in the audience of a five-day rain dance; Tsalatitse was pointed out to me in the street; U'k I failed to see or rather recognize during my first visit to Zuñi in August, he was taking part in the *ko'kokshi* when I began to look for him, in the last two of the five days' dance, and then I had to leave Zuñi. On my second visit in December, U'k was dancing again, but this time I saw him without a mask. The child, Laspeke (for Las Vegas), I had several opportunities to watch. Far from adequate, my observations may be nevertheless worth recording, so very little has been recorded at all about the Indian berdache. I hope to continue the study.

To begin with the little boy, he is still dressed as a male, wearing trousers and a shirt; but his shirt is of a considerably longer cut than that of the other little boys, nor is it tucked into the trousers as they sometimes tuck in theirs. Around his neck is a bead necklace, a mixture of commercial and of stone beads, an ornament not altogether commonplace for either little boys or girls. His hair-cut is the usual all round short cut for boys—girls of his age would be growing a lock at the back of the neck. His features are unusually fine and delicate, unusual even in a Zuñi girl, and his facial expression unusually gentle, mild of expression as is the Zuñi of either sex. Whenever I saw him playing about he was with a girl, although boys of his age begin to gang together. "He talks like a girl," I was told. And by that I learned was meant that he used the "expressions" of a girl,[3] their exclamations and turns of speech.[4] A few of these differentiations in the speech of the sexes I collected:

Oh, dear!
Girl: *Hia an'na!* or *An'na!*
Boy: *Cha an'na!*

Oh, lovely or bully!
Girl: *Ho elu!*
Boy: *Cha elu!*

Outch!
Girl: *Hia atu!*
Boy: *Cha kochi'!*

Stop!
Girl: *elesma!*
Boy: *Lesma!*

I don't want to! I'm shy!
Girl: *Hia ati!*
Boy: *Cha ati!*

Oh, I'm so tired!
Girl: *Hish atu ho utechika.*
Boy: *Hish kochi' ho utechika.*

It's awfully cold!
Girl: *Hish itsu' tetse.*
Boy: *Cha itsu' hish tetse.*

Oh, it's very good!
Girl: *Hish ali hekwa alitecha.*
Boy: *Hish ali alitecha.*

Kasineli has the facial expression and the stature of a man. He has the longer stride of a man, but it is slow and ponderous like the Zuñi woman's. During the rain dances he always stood on the roof top behind the old

woman who is the head of his household. He did not wear the American calico petticoat so many of the Zuñi women wear but his dress was in every particular as far as I could see like a woman's, and he wore his black blanket in woman fashion, up around the back of the head, irrespective of the temperature, and falling to the knees.[5] Next to him on the roof top were standing or sitting three or four kinswomen. One of them was an informant of mine. To the *la'mana* in her family she would never refer, although we talked of the subject in general from time to time and we worked together on her family genealogy. Nor would she take me to the house where he lived, the house of her father's sister where her own little son was living and where she had grown up. Her people had tried very hard to dissuade the lad from becoming a *la'mana*, I was told,[6] and I got the impression that in general a family would be somewhat ashamed of having a *la'mana* among its members. In regard to the custom itself there seemed to be no reticence in general and no sense of shame.

Kasineli is a first-class plasterer. So is Tsalatitse—he had been called in to plaster the chimney-place of the room I lived in, by the way. Kasineli is especially good too at pottery. Among the other six *la'mana* my old man informant had known during his lifetime two were noted as skilful weavers of blankets, and two as skilful potters.[7]

It is the *la'mana*, Mrs. Stevenson states, whose special function it is to fetch from To'wa Yalene the clay used in making pottery. This is certainly not so today; anyone may fetch the clay. My elderly informant declared it was never the function of the *la'mana*. At two periods during his memory, however, have the Priests of the Bow endeavored to give a sacred character to the pottery-making, confining it to the first four days of the summer solstice ceremonial, prescribing the firing for the fourth night. Mrs. Stevenson describes this custom without mentioning, however, that it is an innovation.[8] It is possible, it occurs to me, that limiting the fetching of the clay to the *la'mana* may have been prescribed also by these inventive Bow priests. It is possible, but very doubtful I must say until I hear of other religious or quasi-religious functions attaching distinctively to the *la'mana*. I heard of none.

There are myths, however, in regard to "men-women." In a myth reported by Mrs. Stevenson[9] it is the *chaakwena*, a god captured by the *kia'nakwe*, who puts on the *kor'koshi* (*ko'kokshi*), a woman's dress to break his spirit—he is rebelling against taking part in a dance to celebrate his capture. This was the first appearance of a male, say the Zuñi, in women's dress. The *kor'koshi* mask in the *kia'nakwe* dramatization is in woman's dress and is called the *ko'thlama* (ko'lama).[10] Cushing gives a different account of the first appearance of the "man-woman." The first born of the incestuous couple, Siweluhsina and Siweluhsita, the couple who figure so prominently in Zuñi mythology, was "a woman in fullness of contour, but a man in stature and brawn"—a fairly accurate description of the hermaphrodite. And the Zuñi explanation is that

> from the mingling of too much seed in one kind, comes the two-fold kind, *'hlhmon,* being man and woman combined— even as from a kernel of corn with two hearts, ripens an ear that is neither one kind nor the other, but both!

According to Cushing then this "man-woman of the Ka'ka"[11] is the elder sister of the *ko'yemshi,* those sacred antic personages of Zuñi ceremonial, sexually abnormal too, we recall, because "seedless."

I was unable to verify these myths. It was positively denied that the *ko'lamana* was the offspring of *awan tsita* (their mother) as Sewiluhsita is called. He came up with the others (Siweluhsita and Sewiluhsina came up in advance) and he was among those who were lost crossing the river and with them went to *koluwala* to stay there as a *ko'ko* (god). "He was the first *la'mana,* so there would be others." He figures in the *kia'nakwe* dance because together with other *ko'ko* he was taken prisoner by the *kia'nakwe.*

These myths are, I take it, *a posteriori* explanations of the *la'mana.* They may give a sanction to the transformation custom; they do not originate it. But this matter of possible relationship between the *la'mana* and supernatural function or office needs further study.[12] Meanwhile we should note that the part of the *ko'lamana* appears to be usually taken by a *la'mana.* We'wha took it. Kasineli has taken it. In recent years,[13] however, it has been played by one who is not a *la'mana,* not a "man-woman," but rather a "woman-man" so to speak. Nancy is called in fact, in a teasing sort of way, "the girl-boy," *katsotse* (*ka'tsiki,* girl, *otse,* male). Of the *katsotse* I saw quite a little, for she worked by the day in our household. She was an unusually competent worker, "a girl I can always depend on," said her employer. She had a rather lean, spare, build and her gait was comparatively quick and alert. It occurred to me once that she might be a *la'mana.* "If she is," said her employer, "she is not so openly like the others. Besides she's been too much married for one." She was, I concluded, a "strong-minded woman," a Zuñi "new woman," a large part of her male, as Weininger would say.

It is because they like woman's work, is the reason that has always been given me both in Zuñi and among the Rio Grande pueblos for the existence of the "man-woman." At Zuñi I was also told, one of my if the household were short on women workers a boy would be more readily allowed to become a *la'mana*. It is always insisted upon that there is never any compulsion upon him to become one.

Of the nine *la'mana* known to my aged interpreter, two had married men, *i. e.*, lived with men as their wives. One of these *la'mana* had been known to my younger Zuñi acquaintances. He was described as effeminate looking—"pretty," like a woman. The families of both parties were said to have objected to the "marriage." The "marriage" was discussed with me as an economic arrangement, and with not the slightest hint of physical acts of perversion on the part of either "husband" or "wife." It seemed to me at the time that the utter obliviousness to that point of view was due to ignorance or innocence, not to reticence.[14] On questions of sexual intercourse the Zuñi, I would say, is naturalistic, not reticent. Nevertheless it is not at all unlikely that this oblivious manner was assumed to check further discussions —for reasons I do not know.

Although the *la'mana* U'k was, I gathered on my first visit, somewhat effeminate looking, he was not married. (Here I should say that Tsalatitse is not effeminate looking. Like Kasineli he is tall and walks with a long, heavy stride.) U'k was teased, I was told, by the children, and he would answer them back like a child. He walks too more like a child than either an adult man or an adult woman, "flighty like," with short, nervous steps. In short he is an undeveloped kind of person. A careful and reliable woman described him as a simpleton.

He is, nevertheless, one of the dancers, for he was initiated into the *ko'tikili*,[15] as are all *la'mana*, just like other boys.[16] The night I saw U'k dancing during the *sha'lako* ceremonial he was in the *chaakwena* dance, that is with the set of dancers from the *uptsana kisitsine*.[17] He was clothed in the ordinary woman's dress and buckskin leggings plus the usual Hopi dance blanket. He had a downy white feather in his hair, otherwise his hair was dressed in the regular woman's style, bang and turned up queue. He came in to the house fourth in the line of dancers but soon fell out of line and danced separately, opposite the line. Representing a female personage, as I was told he did—that is the position he would naturally take. Before the dancers withdrew, he took a place in the line again, number six. His dance step was much less vigorous than the others; but that is true too of normal males personating "goddesses." U'k is not as tall as the other *la'mana*, his stature is more that of a woman than a man. His features, however, are masculine. Their expression in this dance was that of animal-like dumb patience.

When U'k fell out of line the audience, an audience mostly of women with their children, girls, and a few old men, grinned and even chuckled, a very infrequent display of amusement during these *sha'lako* dances.[18] "Did you notice them laughing at her?" my Cherokee hostess asked me on my return. "She is a great joke to the people—not because she is a *la'mana*, but because she is half-witted."

Neither U'k nor the other two *la'mana* are members of any of the esoteric fraternities. Of the other *la'mana* my aged informant had known one, and one only belonged to a fraternity, the Bedbug fraternity.

When prepared for burial the corpse of a *la'mana* is dressed in the usual woman's outfit, with one exception, under the woman's skirt a pair of trousers are put on.[19] "And on which side of the graveyard will he be buried?"[20] I asked, with eagerness of heart if not of voice, for here at last was a test of the sex status of the *la'mana*. "On the south side, the men's side, of course. *Kwash lu* [21] *otse tea'me* (Is this man not)?" And my old friend smiled the peculiarly gentle smile he reserved for my particularly unintelligent questions.

Notes

Originally published in *American Anthropologist*, N.S., 18 (1916): 521-28. The original footnotes have been numbered consecutively as endnotes.

1. "The Zuñi Indians," *Twenty-first Annual Report Bureau American Ethnology*, p. 37. Three of them became *la'mana* after 1890.
2. U'k "sounds like a man's name," I was told; *ditse* is the ending of a girl's name.
3. The Hopi woman's word of thanks is *eskwali*, the man's *kwa kwi*. (Hough, W., *The Hopi Indians*, p. 115. Cedar Rapids, 1915.)
4. Lowie notes that Assiniboine berdaches "employed the affirmative and imperative particles peculiar to women's speech." (*Anthropological Papers, American Museum of Natural History*, IV, I, p. 42. New York, 1910.) See too Fletcher, A. C. and La Flesche, F., "The Omaha Tribe," p. 132, *Twenty-seventh Annual Report Bureau of American Ethnology* (1905-6).
5. A Zuñi man wears his blanket in summer only when it is chilly and well up over his head and above his knees. In winter it falls lower, leaving his head bare. Indoors as well as out it stays in place around his neck and across his face up to his nose or even eyes. It is a mode of wearing his blanket as irrespective of temperature and as conventional as that of a woman.
6. Mrs. Stevenson who seems to have known his family pretty well states that his mother and grandmother were quite complaisant, but that the grandfather, the elder brother Bow priest, tried to shame the boy out of his intent. (*The Zuñi Indians*, p. 38.)
7. One of them was undoubtedly We'wha, a notable character. (See Stevenson, *The Zuñi Indians*, pp. 37, 310-13, 374.)
8. *Ib.*, p. 150.
9. *Ib.*, p. 37.
10. *Ib.*
11. "Zuñi Creation Myths," *Thirteenth Annual Report Bureau of American Ethnology*, pp. 401-413.
12. Suggestive in this connection is Jochelson's theory of the "transformed men" of the Chukchee and Koryak. "I think abnormal sexual relations [of five *irka' la'ul* among the 3,000 Kolyma Chukchee, two were "married to other men"] have developed under the influence of the ideas concerning shamanistic power, which the 'metamorphosed' men obtain from the spirits at whose bidding and with whose help the change of sex is accomplished. These beliefs have found fertile soil in individuals of abnormal physical and psychical development." ("The Koryak," pp. 754-5. *Memoirs American Museum Natural History*, vol. VI, pt. II. Leiden and New York, 1908.) See too Parsons, E. C. (Main, John), *Religious Chastity*, pp. 310-1. New York, 1913.

    The Franciscan Fathers refer quite incidentally to the Navajo *na'dle* (he changes) men skilled in the arts and industries of both men and women. (*An Ethnologic Dictionary of the Navaho Language*, p. 292. St. Michaels, Arizona, 1915.) Of any supernatural function or trait attaching to these "hermaphrodites" there is no mention.
13. The *kia'nakwe* ceremonial is quadrennial. It was last performed in November, 1915. On November 17 the *kia'nakwe* prepared their plumes, on November 18 they came in from the south and danced in front of their *kiwitsine*, the *chu'pawa*, where they spent the night. November 19 they danced until the following sunrise.
14. It is a pity Mrs. Stevenson felt called upon to be so reticent. "There is a side to the lives of these men which must remain untold" is all she vouchsafes. (*The Zuñi Indians*, p. 38.) The *la'mana* who was married to a man she mentions, but she refers to the couple merely "as two of the hardest workers in the Pueblo and among the most prosperous."

Stating that the *la'mana* never marry women and seldom, it is understood, have any sexual relations with them, she reports that We'wha was reputed to be the father of several children, his paternity in one case at least being undoubted.

15. The initiation takes place between seven and eleven, the age falling necessarily uncertainly because the ceremonial takes place quadrennially. At any rate this age is prior to that when female dress is definitely assumed, about twelve. Nevertheless, judging from the youngster now qualifying as a *la'mana*, a boy is marked down for one year sooner, and he is initiated into the *ko'tikili* in the knowledge that he is to become a *la'mana*.

16. Girls are not initiated as a regular thing into the *ko'tikili*. There are only four women in it now—a married woman with children, two older widows, a much married but now husbandless woman, the *katsotse* I have already referred to.

    Two reasons for not initiating girls as well as boys were given me at different times by my old man informant. Girls would not talk as boys would of what they saw. So there was no need to initiate them to keep their mouths shut. So much for his offhand bit of rationalism. When I pressed him for his tradition he related that in the first days women were taken into the *ko'tikili*. These were the days when the *ko'ko* themselves came and went between the Pueblo and *ko'luwala*. The women among the *ko'ko* fell in love with them and unwilling to be left behind accompanied them to *ko'luwala*. Lonesome there, they wanted to be brought back to the *ashiwi*. Such flightiness was too much for the *ko'ko* and so the women were no longer admitted into the *ko'tikili*.

    The reason for taking women into the *ko'tikili* is to me still obscure. In her earliest publication on Zuñi Mrs. Stevenson states that the female initiates have to take a vow of celibacy for life and that as a woman member grows old she chooses her successor. In her later publication Mrs. Stevenson omits these statements. I have been told that if a girl were frightened by a bad dream she might be initiated, or, if sick, she might choose to go into the *ko'tikili* instead of one of the fraternities. (*Cf. The Zuñi Indians,* p. 65.) If not initiated under these circumstances, she would die.

17. To that *kiwitsine* he therefore belongs.

18. Aside from the merriment produced by the *ko'yemshi,* the only other show of amusement I saw was called forth by the little boys in the *hemishi'kwe* dance, boys who had their faces painted white and wore a *pitone* to represent female figures.

19. Noted too by Mrs. Stevenson, *The Zuñi Indians*, pp. 312-3.

20. In the center of the graveyard, one of the few Spanish relics in Zuñi, stands a large wooden cross. It forms the boundary line for this mortuary division of the sexes. "Why do you make the division?" I asked my old man informant. "Because we do not pray to the women for rain, only to the men."

21. Personal pronouns showing sex are lacking in Zuñi.

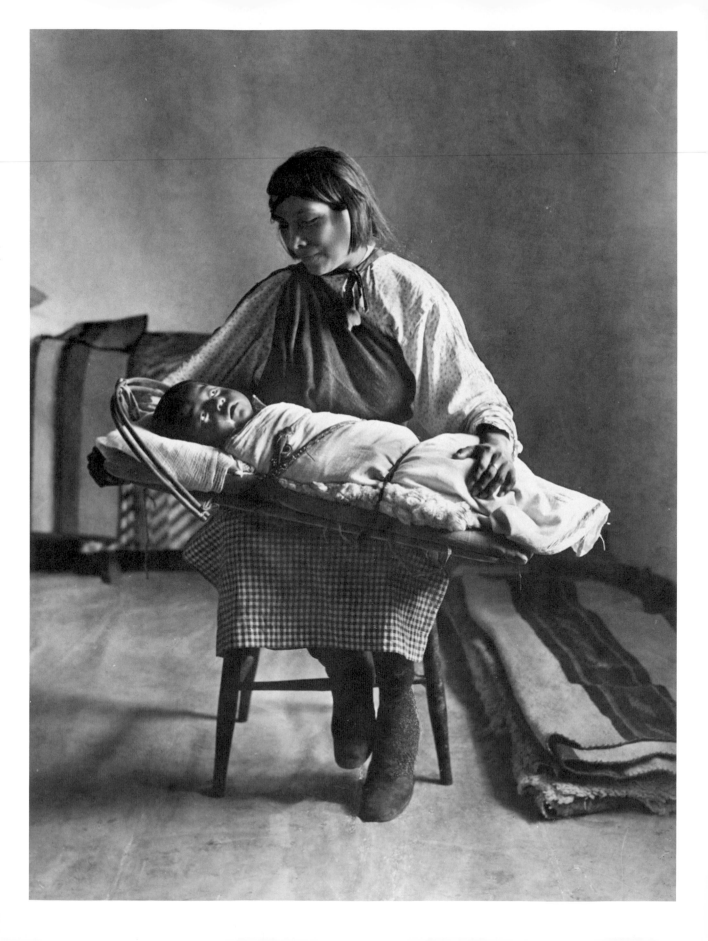

Nativity Myth at Laguna and Zuñi

During a visit to Laguna in February, 1918, I had noticed in the church a model in miniature of the Nativity group. Jesus, Mary and Joseph, the ox and the mule, were represented, and there was a large flock of sheep. José or Tsiwema or Tsipehus,[1] the "sextana," was one of my Laguna informants, and, on asking him the meaning of the crib, he narrated as follows:—

> The baby (*uwak*) José Crito, god's child (*hus*[2] *ka iach*, "god his child") was brought from a far country by his father José and his mother Mari.[3] They took the journey about the time he was going to be born. He was born in a stable. A big fire, a big star, came down from the sky. There was an ox in the stable. When he was born, the ox came there. He blew[4] on the baby. A little after a shepherd (*shtura*) came. That is the reason the priest put the sheep there. That was the way he was born. He went from there to another town, to the king's house (*re gama*), his mother and father and himself, on a horse. He grew up at the king's house. After he had grown up, the others, the Jews (*Uriu*), were not satisfied with him. They were going to kill him. There were three brothers, three children of god; but this one born in the stable was the leader.[5] They were hunting everywhere for him to kill him. One of the Jews asked the middle (*tsunatseiche*) brother which was Jesus. The Jew said, "Which one is it?" He said, "I am not going to tell you." They said, "Yes, you must tell us." So they bribed him. So another party of Jews came into his house. They were all sitting at the table, and still they kept asking which one was it. He was sitting in the north direction. "That's he." So they took him. "Wait a little," he said. "Wait a little, my brothers [*tiumu temishe*]! Which one of you has been given some money?" — "None of us." The one sitting at the east end of the table was the one that had been bribed. "You are the one, you have been paid some money. Now I am going away. I am going up to Konamats ['place of being thankful'].[6] So they took him out of the room. They stood up a cross (*shukasetse*). He was a spirit

Facing Page:

A Laguna mother with her baby on a cradleboard, ca. 1920. Photograph by Herman S. Hoyt. Courtesy of the Museum of New Mexico, Negative no. 72594.

(*kokimun*). So it took some time for them to get ready. When god's child made everything ready, they nailed him to the cross through the middle of his hands. There was one who could not see. There was another who was lame, so his brother carried him on his back. They pierced him through the heart. "Now all is ready," said the Jews. They made the blind man and the lame man pierce his heart. When they pierced him, the blood spurted everywhere. In this way (that is the reason why) from the splattered blood all living beings came, horses and mules and all creatures. The man that was lame got up and walked, and the blind man could see, because they had been spattered with the blood. So at last they dug a hole and stood up the cross. They dug the hole so deep, that the cross could never be taken up. They buried him in this deep hole; they threw dirt and rocks on him, some of the rocks so big that they could hardly lift them; still they threw them in. They buried him. The first day, the second day, he was still buried; the third day he was to leave his grave. He went up to Konamats, back to his father, God. The Jews kept shooting upwards. His father was glad he came back up, so they would live there together in Konamats. The season when he was treated so mean is coming back again. Tomorrow is the first day of mass (*misa*). For seven weeks (*domik*) I have to ring the bell. On the sixth (seventh?) Sunday (*domiku*) it will be *kuitishi*. On the seventh Sunday it is coming back to the same time he went up to heaven. On the Wednesday before *kuitishi* will be the covering (*kaitamishe*).[7] All the people come in to take a turn watching. It is covered Wednesday (*tsuna kaiich*), Thursday (*shuwewise*), Friday (*hienis*). On Saturday (*sauwawu*) it is uncovered. He goes back to his father. It will be *kucheachsi*.[8] That is all (*hemetsa*).

At Zuñi I had frequently asked for a tale (*telapnane*) about the *santu*; but until I asked Klippelanna,[9] none was forthcoming.[10] Klippelanna narrated as follows:—

In the West there lived a Mexican girl (*ellashtoki sipaloa*) who never went out. She staid all the time in her own house. She would sit where the sun shone in. The sun impregnated her ("gave her a child").[11] At this time the soldiers were guarding her.[12] One of the soldiers saw her, and said to the others, "The one we are guarding is pregnant. If she does such things, what is the use of guarding her? Let us kill her!" The next day in the morning she was to die. That evening the Sun by his knowledge (*yam anikwana*) came into her room, and said, "To-morrow you are to die." — "Well, if it is to be, I must die," she said. He said, "No, I won't let you die, I will get you out." The next morning early by his knowledge he lifted her up out of the window.[13] "Now go to where you are to live." So she went on till she came to a *sipaloa* planting. She said, "What are you planting?" He said, "Round stones [*akyamowe*]." Because he did not answer right, she did something to the seed, and his corn did not come up. She went on a little ways, and she came to another one planting. She asked him what he was planting. He said, "I am planting corn and wheat." Because he answered her right, she did nothing to his seed, and they all came up. Then the soldiers found she was gone, and they came on after her. They asked the first man if he had seen a girl coming. He said, "Yes, she has just gone over the hill." They said, "Well, we must be nearly up with her, we will hurry on." So they went on over the hill, and they saw no one. They came to another little hill, and they could not see her. They came to a river, and it was very deep. They cut some poles, and they said, "We'll see how deep it is." They stuck the poles down, and they said, "It is too deep. There is no use in hunting any more for her." So they turned back. But the girl had crossed the river, and went on until she came to Koluwela, and there she lay in (*chawasha*). She had twins. The pigs and the dogs kissed (*tsulpe*) her. That is why the pigs and the dogs have children. The mules would not kiss her. That is why the mules have no children. They came on to Itiwonna (middle, i.e., Zuñi). At Koluwela they all (the mother and twins) became *topo'hi* (another sort of person), they became stone.[14] When they had the dances (at Zuñi), she did not care to see them. She did not like their dances. They had the *hematatsi*. She liked that dance. So she went on to Hakuk (Acoma), because *hematatsi*[15] was a dance of Hakuk. She lives there to-day. The elder sister (*an kyauu*), i.e., of the twins, is here. The younger (*an hani*) went south to where the other Zuñi (*ashiwi*) live. *Lewi*.

The elder sister (*an kyauu*), I learned from one of the paramount *ashiwanni*, had been kept by Naiuchi, famous half a century ago as priest (*shiwanni*) of the north, and *apilashiwanni awan mosi* (bow-priests, their director). From his house the *santu* had been taken to the house where she now lives, a house on the south side.[16] Naiuchi was *kyakyalikwe*, of the Eagle clan, and the present abode of the *santu* belongs to a child of the Eagle; i.e., the paternal clan was Eagle. (It is a house of the Frog clan [*takyakwe*]). For some time a certain Eagle clan family has been trying to get possession of the *santu*. It is assumed that she belongs to the Eagle clan.

In other words, the *santu* has been put into the pattern of the Zuñi fetiches (*ettowe*), which are clan property. Unlike them, she is not kept secreted; but, like them, she is a source of light in the sense of life (*tekohanna*). "All want *tekohanna* from her." And she is also a specific for rain. After a dry season, she will be carried around the fields, as she was two years ago, in the course of her ceremonial (*satechia*). "The *santu* is a *shiwanni*' (rain-priest).

The *santu* is likewise a direct agent of fertility or reproduction. Four days after the winter solstice she lies in (*santu chalia*) for four days; and small clay images of the domestic animals, of bracelets, rings, etc., are placed around her; and to them all she is supposed to give increase during the year.[17] A similar practice has been noted at Acoma.[18] At Laguna there is a practice of making small dough images of animals (*ushumini*), but these representations are merely baked and eaten. The existence of any ceremonial point of view in connection with them was in general[19] denied; and the practice of making clay images in connection with the saint appears, according to my Laguna informants, not to occur. The saint is connected with reproduction, however, according to a Zuñi informant[20] who had grown up in Acoma, and had visited Laguna only last year. The night before the *santu chalia*,[21] said this man, men were free "to plant seeds" in any woman they met. The practice was "to make more children." Resulting offspring were accounted the saint's children. "That is why the saint has so many children."[22]

One more function of the Zuñi *santu*. She is a source of omen (*teliuna*),[23] telling "what will happen." She does "tricks" (*iatsuman*). If the ground looks "dry" around her house (*an kyakwin*),[24] as her bower in the *satechia* may be called, there will be a drought; if the ground is grassy, there will be rain. To a girl to whom something is going to happen the saint's clothes in the *satechia* would look ugly. One year, during the *satechia*, there appeared on her person spots of blood, and in the dance two men were shot. "Last year," narrated my informant, "the first day of the *satechia* when I looked at the *santu*, her eyes were all right; but the second day they were rolling, like the dead. They told me it was a *teliuna*. That winter my cousin died of pneumonia, alone in a sheep-camp, and for three days the sheep were by themselves."[25]

Nothing corresponding to the story of Jesus as heard at Laguna have I been able to find at Zuñi. Stevenson frequently refers to Poshaiyanki as the Zuñi "culture-hero." The myth she gives appears somewhat reminiscent of the Christ myth,[26] and her statement that on the feather-sticks offered to Poshaiyanki a cross figure, appears significant. I learned but little about Poshaiyanki feather-sticks except that all fraternity members do plant feather-sticks to him at the winter-solstice ceremonial. The very existence of Poshaiyanki was unknown to my non-fraternity informants,[27] and denied by one fraternity informant, who never hesitated to lie when he wished to conceal a fact. On the other hand, Klippelanna, when questioned about Poshaiyanki, narrated as follows:—

Poshaiyanki was a "raw person" (*kyapen bo*). He was a man of magic (*aiuchi*). All the fraternities (*tikyawe*) belong to him. Some time in the beginning he came out with all the fraternities. He went all over the country to different towns, and he made all the things for them to do in their fraternities.

Zuni women with olla and child returning from their daily trip to the river. Courtesy of the Museum of New Mexico, Negative no. 14593.

He went all over the world. He got to Lea.[28] When he got to Lea, Lea said to him, "Now you are a great man, you are *aiuchina, kyapen ho*, and do things nobody else can do. Now, to-morrow you and I will do tricks (*iatsuman*) to each other." Lea was tall, and Poshaiyanki was short. "To-morrow, when the sun comes out, the sun will shine on one of us first; that is the one who will win." Lea said to him, "All right!" He had parrot tail-feathers (*lapopon*).[29] In the morning they both stood together, looking to where the sun would rise. When the sun came out, it did not shine on Lea. It shone first on Poshaiyanki. Then he won.[30] "Now, with all the animals we are going to *iatsuman*," he said to him. "All right!" he said. So Lea asked him to be first. He said he would not be the first. "You will be the first," he said to him, "because it was you who wanted to try it." So Lea began. And he called all the animals that belonged to him,—sheep, horses, mules, pigs, chickens. So all gathered together. He told Poshaiyanki to try it. "Now, you try it,"—"All right! I am but an Indian,"[31] he said. So he called all the birds, eagles, hawks, wild turkeys, all kinds of birds, and all flew to them. He called deer (*nawe*), bear, *hoktitasha* (long tail, i.e., cougar), wolf (*unawiko*), and all the other animals. At last all the animals gathered together where they were, and Poshaiyanki had four times more than Lea. So Poshaiyanki beat him again.[32] *Lewi.*

From my priest informant I learned that Poshaiyanki was the father of the fraternities, and that he had lived at Shipap, which famous starting-point was on this occasion placed at Las Vegas. Poshaiyanki discovered the fraternities. Through him they had their animals and birds and medicines.[33] When he talked to the people, those in front heard more plainly than those sitting behind. That is why some fraternity members know more than others. After he had told them everything, he was lost. He did not die. He went through the earth.[34]

Notes

Originally published in the *Journal of American Folk-Lore* 31 (1918):256-63. The original footnotes have been renumbered consecutively as endnotes.

1. Meaning "God's Ear." Since José has been sexton, according to his own account, for more than half a century, since he is also the *shiwanna* (thunder) *cheani*, one of the two surviving medicine-men of Laguna, the nickname appears singularly appropriate, and yet it was given him for quite another than the obvious reason. When he was courting the girl who was to be his second wife, his prospective mother-in-law, a Zuñi, referred to him as a very rich man, boasting that he had come to the house wearing a silver belt and *sipe hus*, here meaning "godlike ear-rings."

2. *Hus* (*yus*) is associated with the sun. "*Osach* [Sun] was sent by naishdya [father] *yus*. That is the reason all look up to him as one with authority [*ityetsa*]." In Keresan mythology the sun is a secondary creation.

3. From another informant I got the terms *Maria Santichuma* and *Esu Christu.*

4. *Gisach* (*chishatsa*) It is the same term as that used for blowing on the feather-sticks or other sacred objects. It corresponds to the Zuñi rite of *yechu*, although at Zuñi the breath is ordinarily drawn in, whereas at Laguna, according to one informant, it is expelled.

5. *Yanitseiche. Yani* is the usual term for "chief;" e.g., the *osach* (sun) *cheani* among the medicine-men is said to be *yani.*

6. *Konama*, "thanks." Wenimats, a place said at Laguna to be west of Zuñi (the Hopi identify it with St. John's), is the "heaven" of native theory. On being questioned, the *sextana* opined that *konamats* and *wenimats* were the same, meaning perhaps equivalents.

7. The bell and all the figures in the church are covered with cloth.

8. End or breaking of taboo. Were a masked dancer to break a restriction (e.g., were he to have sexual intercourse during the ceremonial), it would be *cheachsi*. After a birth, continence is required for twelve days. In case of *cheachsi* a medicine-man will be called in to give a purge; otherwise the woman will dry up (*tsipanito*). Compare E. C. Parsons, "Zuñi Death Beliefs and Practices" (AA 18:246).

9. A very garrulous and unusually naïve old man, who is sometimes reputed a witch. He is the fraternity director (*tikya mosi*) of the Little Fire fraternity (*matke tsannakwe*).

10. Sometimes the *santu* was admitted to be Mexican, sometimes it was stated that she had been with them "from the beginning," she came up with them. One of the paramount priests (*ashiwanni*) who asserted the latter origin added that the *santu* had never staid in the church except during her lying-in at the winter-solstice ceremonial.

11. Compare F. H. Cushing, *l.c.,* 429 *et seq.*

12. Men volunteer as soldiers (*sontaluk*) to guard the *santu* during her ceremonial. Analogously, among the Keresans the "war captains" guard the mother (*iyebik, uretseta*).

13. At this point our usually amenable interpreter refused to go on translating. He said that he had heard the story otherwise; that Klippelanna was not telling it right; and that if I told the story wrong, he himself would be held responsible. Asked to particularize, he said that as Klippelanna was telling the story, the domestic animals came to Kôluwela. That was not right; there were no such animals in Koluwela ("god town," where the gods [*koko*] live, and the dead). I argued that it was "ours not to reason why," that all he and I had to do was to take down the story as it was given to us; but I suggested and pleaded in vain. He refused to translate. "No, let us have another story!" he firmly concluded. The story was retold another time, and translated by Margaret Lewis, a non-

Zuñi. Leslie's refusal to translate seemed to me a striking illustration of Zuñi tenacity to pattern; and it calls to mind an opinion of Dr. Kroeber, our most authoritative student of Zuñi, namely, that, although fifty per cent of Zuñi culture may be borrowed from White culture, the Zuñi have so cast what they have taken over into their own patterns, that ninety-nine per cent of their culture may be called indigenous.

14. *Variant:*The *santu* had been a real baby belonging to a Mexican lady; then the *santu* turned into stone. The *santu* was one of the raw people (*kyapenahoi*); i.e., supernaturals.

15. Said to be the *upikaiupona.*

16. In a house on the west side there is said to be another *santu,* one bought from Mexicans. It belongs to the Tansy-mustard clansman who figures in the *molawia* ceremonial.

17. See E. C. Parsons, "Notes on Zuñi," pt. I (MAAA 4:170-171).

18. C. F. Lummis, The Land of Poco Tiempo (New York, 1897), 276.

19. According to one informant, *ushumini* were offered to "animals" before hunting. If the images disappeared, it meant that deer would be killed.

20. He also asserted that clay animals were placed around the saint, both at Acoma and Laguna. At both places, we may note, the saint is male.

21. Kuashe was referring to Christmas Eve, for he also used the Mexican term *nochowena* (*nochebuena*). From this the Zuñi *santu chalia* would appear to be a Christmas rite, *santu chalia* being merely a translation of *la navidad.* It is at *nochowena* that the Zuñi will visit Laguna. At Laguna as well as at Acoma (see E. C. Parsons, "Notes on Acoma and Laguna" [AA 20:162-186]) there is a prolonged Christmas celebration. Beginning Dec. 16, the church-bell is rung each morning about nine o'clock, and mass is said by the *sextana.* Every one counts the days. On Dec. 22, rehearsal of the dances (*Kutanigwia*, "trying") is held at night, —held, it happens, in Jefferson's house, a large house, an *osach* (sun) clan house. Dec. 24, the ninth day, the "great day," after mass at 11 A.M., by the priest, there are Comanche, Eagle and Corn (*yakohanna* or *talawaie*) dances (*katsetia*). Everybody is on hand, eager to see or take part. After midnight mass the dances continue in the church until 2 or 3 A.M. Dec. 25, Comanche, *talawaie*, etc., dances first in church about 11 A.M., and then in the plaza, the Christmas Eve dancers being called upon to dance till sunset.—Dancers from outlying villages, as in 1918 the Eagle dancers, may quit earlier. Private presents of food are made, and there is an interchange of presents—bread, chile, fruit, china, cloth—between *comadres*; i.e., the godmother gives a present to her godchild, and the child's mother, a present to the godmother. Mexicans go singing from house to house, and receive presents of food. *Talawaie (danawaiye)* is danced in the plaza from Dec. 26 through Dec. 29. During these four days children may take part. The last day in particular is made much of. Jan. 1, king day (*lei shashte*), election of governor and officers *(tenientes).* Jan. 6, dances, Comanche, Navaho, etc., at night in different houses in honor of newly-elected officers. Jan. 7, 8, 9, dances (mostly *talawaie*) in the plaza in all the villages for *tenientes*. (Jan. 9, 1918, was stormy, and in consequence the dance was in the church.) Jan. 10 great *fiesta* by Mexicans at Seboyeta.—The dance-place in the church is below the altar, the different sets of dancers taking turns until towards the end all the sets dance at the same time. In 1917-18 there were about twenty dancers in the *talawaie*, men and women dancing in two lines, the sexes alternating. There were six men in the Comanche dance, and two men in the Eagle dance. The delight-makers (*kachale*) are said to appoint the Christmas-time dancers, and none may refuse. Unlike the *katsena* dances, for which new songs are composed, only old songs are sung in the Christmas-time dances. The Comanche and Eagle dancers have a choir.—All the dances are without masks, but formerly in the *talawaie* the women wore squared wooden turkey-befeathered headpieces or tablets (*uteduish.* "on the top"). The older men wear white cotton trousers and shirts; the younger men, their ordinary American clothes, plus high buckskin leggings tied with the woman's hair belt. Comanche dancers wear a head-dress of eagle-feathers and ribbons. The eagle-feather head-dress of the Eagle dancers reaches to the

feet. The faces of the Eagle dancers are painted.

22. This practice was described to a company of Zuñi, and the description amused them just about as it would have amused a company of sophisticated whites. The practice was plainly not Zuñi. Nevertheless at the "big dances" (i.e., the dances in which the people take part),—formerly the scalp-dance and the *owinahaiye*, and to-day the saint's dance (*satechia*,—it lasts two days or more, according to whether any one asks for a repetition), there is always a certain amount of license among the girls. —A Zuñi informant told me he had seen a bereaved Mexican woman praying to the Zuñi *santu* for a child that would live.

23. Compare E. C. Parsons, "Notes on Zuñi," pt. I (MAAA 4:189).

24. Similarly at Laguna the bower in the plaza (*kakati*) to which the *santu* is carried is called *santu gama*. In the anti-sunwise circuit from the church the padre leads, followed in order by the governor (*tapup*), the *sextana*, the *santu* carried by the women, and all the people.

25. Compare beliefs about *achiyelotopa* (M. C. Stevenson, "The Zuñi Indians," RBAE 23:462).

26. The Sia Poshaiyänne myth is in part indubitably Christian (M. C. Stevenson, "The Sia," RBAE 11:65-67).

27. A priest excepted, who stated that non-fraternity persons would not know about Poshaiyanki. This priest also stated that there was no cross on the feather-sticks to Poshaiyanki, and that the fraternity feather-stick on which a face is painted is that which is offered to Poshaiyanki. Note J. W. Fewkes, "Hopi Shrines near the East Mesa, Arizona" (AA 8:367, 368); also Fewkes, "Winter Solstice Ceremony at Walpi" (AA 11:75). Prayer-sticks in the form of a cross for the increase of domestic animals are mentioned, likewise (pp. 72, 75) to the same end the use of clay or wooden images of animals.

28. "King," Leslie translated, quite properly, but much to my surprise. *Lea*, usually pronounced *lei*, is from *rei*, and the word has become at Zuñi a proper name. Leslie had learned its generic meaning, I suspect, from non-Zuñi sources.

29. Such as are worn by the dancers, more particularly the *kokokshi*, in their hair. There is a suggestion here of magical quality in the feathers.

30. Compare "The Sia" (RBAE 11:33-34).

31. *Ho'ite*. Ho'ite appears to be a generic term for any Indian.

32. Compare "The Sia" (RBAE 11:59-65); Father Dumarest, MS. on Cochiti in the Brooklyn Institute Museum. Poshaiyanki becomes Montezuma, and included in the myth is the following unmistakably Christian incident:"Montezuma made a house where none could find him, because he had enemies, and where he could deliberate on what he had to do. He had to reform the unmarried mothers. He made a serpent like a fish with wings. It would go into a house and throw itself upon the mother and child as if to devour them. It lived in a lake, where it became very large. Instead of merely frightening the mothers and children, it ended up devouring them. Montezuma had to confine the serpent to the lake forever."

33. On another occasion the same informant stated that Poshaiyanki also brought sheep, burro, and horses. Having first asserted that nothing at all had come to the Zuñi through the Spaniards, he admitted that the *sipaloa* or *kishdyan* (an old word for "Mexican") had brought wheat and watermelons. Peach-trees were already there when the Zuñi came up, and they brought with them corn and squash.

34. We recall that Koluwela is underground.

*Women planting
waffle gardens at
Zuni, ca. 1911.
Photograph by Jesse
L. Nusbaum.
Courtesy of the
Museum of New
Mexico, Negative no.
43170.*

Increase by Magic: A Zuñi Pattern

On the first day of the winter solstice ceremonial, men plant feather-sticks to the old ones (*aklashinawe*), *i. e.*, the dead, and to the sun; and women to the dead and to the moon. Five days later, men plant to the *koko*, the masked impersonations, and for *utenawe*, property. On this day the saint begins to lie in (*santu chalia*, saint, childbirth) for four days. The night before *santu chalia*, *i.e.*, Christmas eve, small clay figures of sheep, horses, donkeys, cows, chickens, of chili and melons, of bracelets, and of gold and silver coins are placed around the *santu* to be left there during the following four days when they are taken home and kept during the year, or, in case of the animals, buried near the corrals. The people of *shiwanni* (rain priest) houses do not take their figurines to the house of the *santu*, but place them on the *teshkwin* (altar), the *shiwanni* altar, in their own house. Here they also place in clay holders cuttings from peach trees on which are stuck peaches made of corn-meal and colored with a red stone.[1] Subsequently, the peach tree cuttings may be taken back to the orchard and planted. The meal peaches together with meal models of corn ears[2] are eaten by the children. The children believe the peaches have grown over night.

The clay figurines are placed in a shrine hole under the floor. The subterranean shrine I saw was in a room next to the ceremonial room of the *ashiwanni* and near the closet in which masks and other sacrosanct objects were kept. After the stone slab, about 2 feet x 1 foot, was lifted off, the foot-deep shrine appeared as in the diagram (fig. 1).

Fig. 1. Subterranean shrine in onakwe ashiwanni *house, Zuñi.* a, *horse with saddle;* b, *sheep;* c, *bracelet;* d, *gold and silver coins;* e, *feather sticks.*

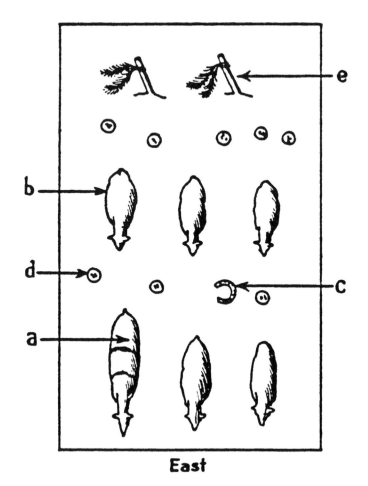

East

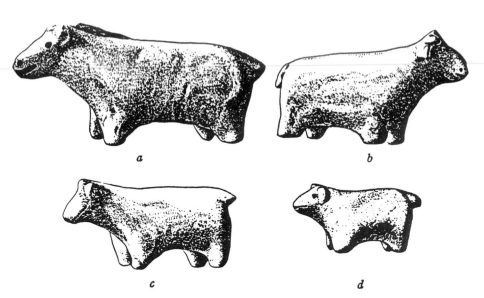

Fig. 2.—Zuñi figurines. In American Museum of Natural History. a, horse (50.2-1211a); b, cow (50.2-1211b); c, sheep (50.2-1211c); d, lamb (50.2-1211d). Size 1/2.

Fig. 3.—Feather-stick for utenawe. *Facet yellow with three black dots. The rest of stick blue (50.2-365e). Size 2/5.*

The figurines were like those figured in fig. 2 which were made for me by a man living in this same *shiwanni* house. The two feather-sticks in the shrine[3] were for *poshaiyanki*, the mythical giver of domestic animals and of wealth (*utenawe*). I am fairly certain that the feather-sticks for *utenawe* (fig. 3) are the same as those for *poshaiyanki*.[4] According to one informant, the *poshaiyanki* sticks are planted at night, the night following the first day of the winter solstice ceremonial—the only sticks planted in night time— according to another informant, they are planted at sunrise,[5] the sunrise following the night all the societies are engaged in curing, the fourth night of the winter solstice ceremonial, the same night the figurines are taken to the *santu* or set out on the altars of the *ashiwanni*.

The figurines and the rite in general is referred to as *itsumawe—santu itsumawe* or *shiwanni itsumawe*. The rite is for the increase of all the objects represented. A rite for the increase of children or the development of an unborn child is also referred to as *itsumawe*. During a dance a woman who has had miscarriages may be given a *wiha* (baby) or doll by a *koko* or masked impersonation. The *wiha* is given more or less privately, perhaps in one of the houses on the dance plaza, to the would-be mother. The *koko* dancer says to the woman,

lil toman ho teapkunan itsumakye
here you I children make *itsuma*

The woman breathes in (*yechu*), sprinkles sacred meal on the *koko*, and gives him some bread. Subsequently the *wiha*, together with the cradle board sometimes given with it, may be carried by the woman secretly under her blanket when she goes outdoors.[6] Once as we were talking

Women grinding corn at Zuni, ca. 1911. Photograph by Jesse L. Nusbaum. Courtesy of the Museum of New Mexico, Negative no. 43239.

of this practice, a little boy, the nephew of my informant, came into the room, and I was told that before his birth the child's grandmother had taken an old *wiha* in her possession and given it to *koyemshi awan tachu* to dress as the mask *hututu* and to give to her expectant daughter. The doll was given to the young woman, herself a *shiwanni*, in the house of her mother's brother on the dance plaza. Of this *itsuma wiha* the little boy was exhibit one; exhibit two was the doll itself, *hututu wiha*. It had been kept as "the heart" of the child, and in this case as in many others enquired into, the family would not think of parting with what appears to be a kind of life token. Were they to sell the *wiha*, the child "it brought would not live."

Human reproduction may be associated also with *shiwanni itsumawe* rites. I heard of one woman at least, who had brought a clay figurine of a baby (*wiha*) to a *shiwanni* winter solstice altar. However, she did not get a baby because she did not go on bringing gifts to the *ashiwanni*.

Is the *itsumawe* ritual of Spanish provenience? Its association at Zuñi as well as at Acoma[7] and Laguna[8] with the *santu* cult and, at Zuñi, with *poshaiyanki* also, a personage associated with Christian lore,[9] is highly suggestive of Spanish origin. On the other hand in the excavations at Hawikuh, one of the Zuñi towns at the coming of the Spaniards, figurines (fig. 4) which are like the modern Zuñi figurines are found, Mr. Hodge tells me, in refuse heaps at all levels, pre-Spanish as well as post-Spanish.[10]

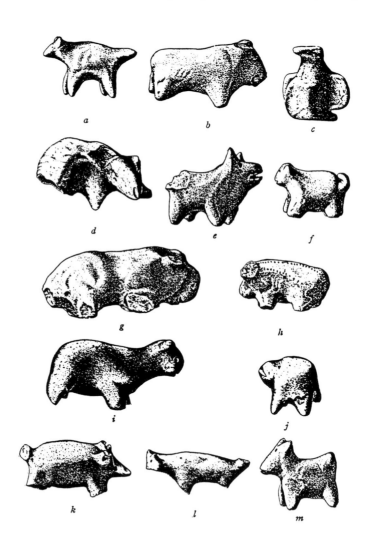

Fig. 4.—Figurines from Hawikuh. In the Museum of the American Indian, Heye Foundation. Notable in b, f, i, j, k, are two perforations indicating that the object was to be hung or attached. In k, the perforations are through the ears, in the others, in chest and under tail. (a-i, size 1/2; j-l, size 5/8; m, size 1/1.)

Moreover, in a prehistoric pueblo in Southern Arizona, Cushing collected a set of figurines (fig. 5) of similar workmanship. Of these Cushing reports that beneath the floor of a hut outside the pueblo were found

Procession of women carrying meal at Zuni, ca. 1920. Courtesy of the Museum of New Mexico, Negative no. 41557.

disposed precisely as would be a modern sacrifice of the kind in Zuñi, the paraphernalia of a herder's sacrifice, namely, the paint-line encircled perforated medicine cup, the herder's amulet-stone of chalcedony, and a group of at least fifteen remarkable figurines. The figurines alone, of the articles constituting this sacrifice, differed materially from those which would occur in a modern Zuñi "New Year Sacrifice" of the kind designed to promote the increase and prosperity of its herds. While in Zuñi these figurines invariably represent sheep (the young of sheep mainly; mostly also females), the figurines in the hut...represented...some variety, I should suppose, of the auchenia or llama of South America.[11]

Not to be overlooked in this connection are the clay figurines of very rough workmanship collected from the Cañon de Chelly in central Arizona and now in the Brooklyn Institute Museum (fig. 6, *a-g*). Figures *a-d* are animals of much the same type as the Hawikuh representations. Figures *e-g* appear to be human. The pecking on them is similar to that on figure 4*b* from Hawikuh.

Fig. 5.—One of eight similar figurines in the Peabody Museum of Harvard University.

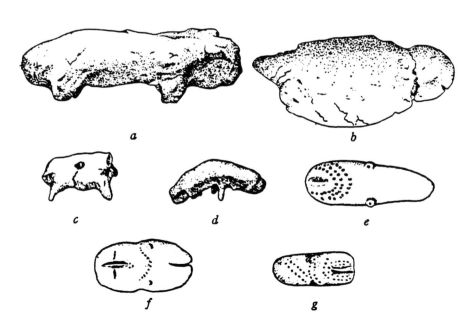

Fig. 6.—Figurines from the Canon de Chelly. In the Brooklyn Institute Museum. a (12288) size 1/3; b (12301) size 1/6; c and d (12296, 12295) size 3/5; e (10722) size 3/5; f (12292) size 3/5; g (12291) size 3/5.

Aside from this archaeological evidence, the *itsumawe* concept takes form at Zuñi in what appears to be distinctly native rituals.

At the stick planting of all the society members at the winter solstice ceremonial, a crook stick (*tapone*) is included. It represents a cane and expresses a desire for longevity.[12] The use of this stick is referred to as an *itsumawe* rite. An upright stick sometimes accompanies the crook. It represents a digging stick (*hetseme*) and as it is used because the offerer "wants to be able to use a digging stick for a long time," it is, I infer, a part of the *itsumawe* ritual.[13]

Again at the close of the winter solstice ceremonial, when the *teshkwi* (taboo, sacred,) is over (*teshkwiha*), and, after the mask *shitsukya* passes the house, the refuse accumulated during the ten days of the *teshkwi* (*pochewe*) is carried out, there appears to be an *itsuma* character to the rites. Whoever goes out first after *shitsukya* has passed—he makes his round before dawn—will get the things of those who are still asleep in the house—(*itiwanna*, middle, *i.e.*, winter solstice, *itsume*, this is called). The next one who goes out will get half the things, the next, a quarter of the things, and so on. (The idea back of this numerical progression is not altogether clear, but I was unable to *préciser*). The refuse or trash is carried out by the man of the hosue. It represents corn, and he stacks it on the ground as he would the corn he brings in from the harvest. The woman of the house carries out ashes which represent meal and, as she would sprinkle meal at the harvest, she sprinkles the ashes on the ground before stacking and then on the stack. Little boys carry fire brands.[14] Everybody in the house will sprinkle the stack and pray to the Sun as follows:

yam iatsume yalakwekya kwa hol tekyalatikya
my finished not whatever done something wrong
el osonakya ho kole hol hona to awanitso
no mind I done whatever we you think about us doing wrong
manamtu
charge

This is a prayer for forgiveness for any violation of the *teshkwi*,[15] but the use of the word *iatsume* in the prayer suggests that the winter solstice ceremonial as a whole may be thought of as a ceremonial[16] for increase.[17]

Staying awake in the societies the night before *koanne* (god going), the last night of the *koko awia* (god coming) ceremonial (the *shalako*) is also referred to as *itsume*—*itsume telinan* (at night). They who succeed in staying awake will get goods (*utenawe*), the property of those who fall asleep.

Notes

Originally published in *American Anthropologist,* N.S., 21 (1919):279-86. The original footnotes have been renumbered consecutively as endnotes.

1. See M. C. Stevenson, "The Zuñi Indians," *Twenty-third Annual Report, Bureau of American Ethnology*, pl. XXXV (1901-2). Stevenson appears to have misinterpreted the meaning of the "offerings" of "thanksgiving."
2. Wheat too may be represented on the altar.
3. The same sticks had been in the shrine for three years.
4. *Cp.* the feather-sticks offered by the Hopi for the increase of sheep. (Solberg, 0., "Über die Bahos der Hopi," p. 68. *Archiv f. Anthropologie*, N.F., vol. IV (1906). That one of the Hopi sticks is in the shape of a cross (pl. XXIII, 30) may not be insignificant in view of the confusion or identification of *poshaiyanki* with Jesus.

    A prayer stick with a cross bound with red wool is offered by the governor of Laguna and his officers.
5. Under a slab in a field by the heads of each society.
6. For a like practice at Cochiti, see Noël, Dumarest, "Notes on Cochiti," *Memoirs, American Anthropological Association,* vol. VI, no. 3.
7. See E. C. Parsons, "Nativity Myth at Laguna and Zuñi." *Journal of American Folk-Lore*, vol. XXXI (1918), p. 260. The rite of increase occurs among the Hopi, who are said to have buried their saint when the Catholics were dispossessed in the Great Rebellion. With no Spanish saint to whom the rite might attach, nevertheless it is with the Spanish importation that the rite is associated. "In almost every Hopi sheep corral there is a place where clay images of the animals are placed as prayers for the increase of domestic animals. These images are commonly made in the Winter Solstice ceremony and in the Warrior festival that follows it" (J. W. Fewkes, "Hopi Shrines near the East Mesa, Arizona," *American Anthropologist*, N.S., vol. VIII [1906], pp. 369-370).
8. Christmas Eve, baskets of figurines of sheep, cattle, horses, pigs, chickens, money, peaches, melons, etc., are taken to the church. Subsequently the figurines are buried, the animal models in the corrals, the fruit models in the gardens, and the models of money, etc., under the house floor. The rite is considered "Mexican".
9. "Nativity Myth at Laguna and Zuñi," pp. 261-3. *Poshaiyanki* is a giver of the Spanish brought domestic animals, but in myth he is also associated with deer and native wild animals. An early "culture hero" may well have been assimilated with a Montezuma–Jesus personage. The *suskikwe* or *tsaniakwe* (hunters' society) furnish an example of transition of interest in the wild animals to interest in the domesticated. This society makes medicine for traders to the Navajo, traders in *utenawe*, horses, beads, etc. The *utena awan lamma* (valuables, their stick) was also identified for me as the stick the society offers for a hunt.
10. In a bin in a house at Hawikuh has been discovered a collection of animal figurines together with rude models of what the Zuñi workmen consider melons, peaches, and coins.
11. F. H. Cushing, "Preliminary Notes on the Origin, Working Hypothesis and Primary Researches of the Hemenway Southwestern Archaeological Expedition," pp. 177-8, in *Compte Rendu du Congrès International des Américanistes*, Berlin, 1888. Quoted also in *Tenth Annual Report, Bureau American Ethnology*, p. 682 (1888-9).

    An outline of a figurine in the same set is reproduced in a report by Washington Matthews on the Hemenway collection in *Publications of the National Academy of Sciences*, vol. VI, p. 156, Seventh Memoir.

12. *Cp.* Solberg, p. 65.
13. Stevenson refers to *poshaiyanki* sticks planted at the winter solstice ceremonial to which are attached a miniature cane for longevity and a miniature corn planter for increase of corn. ("The Zuñi Indians," pp. 119-20.)
14. As *shulawitsi*, a boy mask, carries a fire brand.
15. There are several restrictions during the winter solstice ceremonial. There is no telling how a child, for example, may have broken one. Among other taboos a light may not be made out doors. I heard of a little boy of four who scratched a match and whose feather-sticks had therefore to be replanted.
16. It is said specifically that if *pochewe* is taken out prematurely they will not get rain, but this is the usual sanction for almost any ceremonial observance.
17. Unless *iatsume* refers strictly to the rivalry in staying awake all night. There is some obscurity about the use of the two terms—*itsume* and *iatsume*. The former appears to apply to increasing by magic, the latter to competing in magic as when groups or individuals vie in producing rain or in assembling animals or in causing or curing disease.

Mothers and Children at Laguna

Wana's baby was two weeks old on my last (1918) visit to Laguna, and as the baby lay in her behooded board cradle on the floor or, still in her compartment, on the lap of her mother or her great-aunt, our talk led naturally from her and her short experience to ways with babies in general. Like other Pueblo Indian babies, she had been taken outdoors and presented to the gods. On the fourth morning of her life, before sunrise, one of the two surviving medicine-men of Laguna, the *shiwanna* (thunder) *cheani* came to the house and laid out on the floor of the upper room of the two-storied house his altar paraphernalia. Wana made for me the following diagram of the altar:—

South.

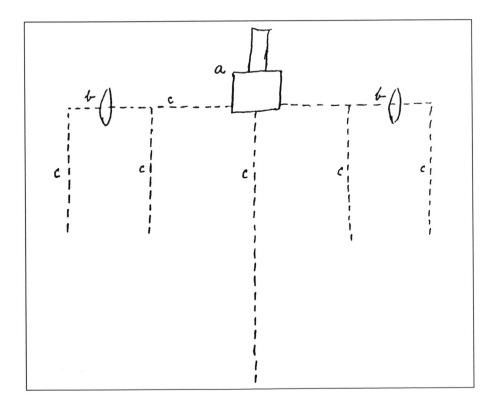

a = iyetik.   *b = ihish* (flint knife).   *c* = meal line.

The *iyetik* is a fetich or symbol of the deity within the earth, a deity who is to the Keresans a source of being and the most revered of all their supernaturals, *naiya* (mother) *iyetiku*. The symbolic *iyetik* is an ear of corn wrapped with unspun cotton and set in a little buckskin cap. When set out on an altar—the only time it is exposed—it is dressed with feathers and encircled with a string of precious beads—turquoise and white shell beads, together with olivella or abalone shells. On either side of the *iyetik* in our diagrammatic altar is a flint knife. The flint knives serve in this case, I surmise, as in other cases of ceremonial usage, as a guard to the *iyetik* or altar against witches or evil spirits.[1] The central line of meal is a roadway for the *kopishtaiya*, the benevolent supernaturals, probably in this case more particularly for *naiya iyetik*, to come in by. Usually on altars the meal road leads from the east, the altar facing the east. I could not learn why in this instance the characteristic position was changed. In myth, to be sure, *naiya iyetik* lives at *shipopolima* (in the north).

In the diagram of the altar a medicine-bowl should have been represented, as from it, out of his shell cup,[2] the *shiwanna cheani* gave Wana a drink, and from it with his eagle feathers he also asperged mother and child, two little rites of constant occurrence in Pueblo Indian ceremonials. According to one informant there should also be a crook stick on the altar, as with it the *cheani* would sprinkle meal on the infant.

After the preliminaries at the altar, the order of which I could get with no certainty, the *cheani* took mother and child out on the southern terrace of their house. With them went Wana's aunt (her mother's sister; her mother is dead),[3] Getsitsa, the head of Wana's household,[4] an old lady whom, in accordance with Keresan kinship terminology, Wana calls *naiya*, mother. Out on the terrace Gestitsa, facing the east, said this prayer:[5]—

shauau naiya osach waii gaiutse waniumasi she shkutsipa
Now mother [*iyetik*] sun this morning I am going out I want
samaak nitunigunishe[6] *sashgama sukiutsi eme shkutsipa nitunigunishe*
my daughter grow up daily all the time this want grow up
du hiname osach hano dieshe Ges.[7]
this myself sun clan thus.

"Now Mother [*iyetik* understood], Sun, this morning I am going out. I want my daughter [the infant] to grow day by day. Thus all the time I want her to grow. I myself am of the Sun clan. I am Ges."

After sprinkling meal on the ground and making four times a circular gesture with both hands raised, palms upward, to the East and drawn back, a ritualistic invitation to the *kopishtaiya*, and after breathing on the infant,[8] the *cheani* prayed as follows:—

towiki naiya naishdiya toheme tauwa nawigesineshe
Here give mother [iyetik] father [Sun] that is all good relationship
tsityu tsitawa hanonatakonishe emitoa shkutsipa naiya naishdiya
of value goodness people multiplying this way want mother father
towik⁹ iani cheowa taame shkutsipa.
take road take this ask want.

"Here I give you the child, Mother *iyetik*, Father Sun. That is all. Good and valuable relationship (*i.e.*, of kin and clan), goodness, increase of people. Such I want. Mother *iyetik*, Father Sun, take the road [of the child's life]. This I ask and want."

Two ceremonial requirements in connection with or subsequent to the rite should be mentioned. Before the rite the mother's hair has been washed—a hair wash is commonly required before Pueblo Indian ceremonials—and before the rite and after, for twelve days after the birth, the woman is expected to be continent. In case of violation (*cheachsi*) she would dry up (*tsipanito*), *i.e.*, die,[10] unless she were given a purge by the medicine-man.

In this presentation rite there was no reference to naming the infant, and when I made the acquaintance of the baby she had not as yet been given any name. How she would get her Indian name I did not hear from Wana,[11] but there was talk of how in course of time she would be given an "American" name in baptism at the Catholic church. Water would be put to her head and salt to her lips and the Spanish godparent institution would be entered into. Every Christmas thereafter her godmother, her mother's *comadre*, would give her a present—and her mother would give a return present to her godmother.

Laguna children, like other Pueblo Indian children, receive other presents, presents of a more distinctively native character. While a ceremonial by masked dancers or *katsena* is under way, parents will ask one of the dancers, perhaps a kinsman, to make a bow and arrow or an *auwak* (a baby) for their child—bow and arrow for a boy, *auwak* for a girl. The parent supplies the materials, and in using them the dancer says a prayer for the good of the child. As among the Zuñi or the Hopi the dolls represent the

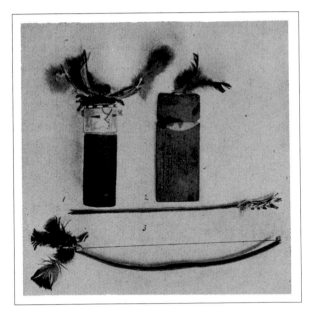

From *Man*, vol. 17, no. 3, March 1919. Courtesy of Laboratory of Anthropology of the Museum of New Mexico.

katsena themselves. Fig. 1 represents a male impersonator called *nawish*. It was made in the autumn of 1917, during the *yakohanna* or corn dance, and until my visit a few months later it had been standing on a shelf of the child's house. Fig. 2 represents a *kuchinninaku* or girl *katsena*. It was given me by the little girl who had been playing with it. Fig. 3 represents the *ishtua* (arrow, bow understood) given by the *katsena* to boys, to boys past infancy; to baby boys such a gift, it is believed, would bring with it life-long bad temper.

By an elderly informant, *comadre* by the way in eight families, was sung for me the two following lullabies:—

hawi hawi hawi-i amu maku shuwiminatse uwitsimikia aihamakoshewi
Who who who dear be quiet turquoise baby board on hush
showaini ni e a shuwiminatse uwitsimikia.
take care turquoise baby board on.

> "There, there, there,
> Dear be quiet,
> On a turquoise[12] baby board
> Hush, take care
> On a turquoise baby board."

hawi hawi hawi kuchinninaku tsekuma shutsaiawita tsekuma
Who who who girl why angry why
shunashgatsita amu kuchinninaku tuwa tuwa chikutuemetse tuwa
captious, cross dear girl here here wild roses here
tuwa gaitayadyama shannakura kwie chukwoya amu.
here moonlight flowers give take dear.

> "There, there, there
> Girl, why are you angry
> Why are you captious, dear girl?
> Here, here are wild roses
> Here, here is moonlight
> The flowers, take them, dear."

Facing Page:

Mrs. Sarracino and children and Mrs. Shije braiding her hair. Laguna, 1935. Photograph by T. Harmon Parkhurst. Courtesy of the Museum of New Mexico, Negative no. 2879.

My singer was a knowing and communicative acquaintance. Unlike the younger generation at Laguna, she was interested in past or passing customs. Various beliefs and practices in connection with mothers and children of which she told seem worth recording. If a pregnant woman

*Laguna water carrier,
ca. 1917. Courtesy of
the Museum of New
Mexico, Negative no.
21529.*

sits with her back to the sun the placenta will "stick." Hence when the placenta is retarded someone present is apt to say, "Perhaps she sat with her back to the sun and the sun baked her back." Twins may be due to witchcraft. A witch will make two balls of earth wet by urine and roll the balls in the direction of the woman who has urinated. Hence urinating in the road is disapproved of.[13] If a baby is born with teeth it is a sign that before his birth his mother has looked at a snake. Parental indiscretions of this kind are the stock explanation of congenital deformities at Zuñi.[14] My Laguna informant explained only one case in this way, the case of a child born with a piece out of his ear, the explanation being that his father had gone out shooting during the pregnancy.

Soon after the birth, perhaps even the first day, ashes will be rubbed on the child,[15] rubbed in the form of a cross on forehead, on chin, and on legs—witches dislike ashes. After hearing about this witchcraft prophylaxis I asked Wana and Getsitsa if the baby had been rubbed yet with ashes. "No," said Wana, "but *naiya* has been thinking about it." The next morning they told me the ashes had been rubbed on—rubbed on the forehead, as I saw when they showed me the baby, just as on Zuñi babies. The ashes were not rubbed on in the form of a cross, nor were they rubbed anywhere else on the body.

There is, or rather was, said my elderly informant, a prejudice at Laguna against clipping a boy's hair, a prejudice probably characteristic, I may add, of all the Pueblo Indians. Once a godchild who was out herding sheep had lice in his hair, so "they" cut it short. His mother felt greatly distressed, and exclaimed to her *comadre*, "They scattered my blood and my health to the four winds!"

Formerly at Laguna, in the days when there were no tables and the household formed a circle around the bowls on the floor, each kneeling on the left knee, none would drink until eating was accomplished. After the meal a senior might touch the breast of a child and say, "Now if all your food has gone down you may drink." Then or at any other time when a senior asked a child to bring him or her a drink the child was expected to stand with arms folded until the senior said, *Shetunii*, "May you grow tall!" *Tauwa* (good, *i.e.*, "thanks") responded the junior.

Laguna women selling pottery at the railroad. Photograph by Frederick H. Maude. Courtesy of the Southwest Museum, Negative no. N20269.

Notes

Originally published in *Man* no. 18, March 1919, pp. 34-38. The original footnote symbols have been converted to numerals and numbered consecutively as endnotes.

1. Spear points figure among the Sia in what appears to be a rite of exorcism after a birth. Stevenson, M.C.:"The Sia," p. 139, XI (1889-90).—*Ann. Rep. Bur. Ethnol.*
2. Shells are used for medicine-water among the Sia, likewise among the Zuñi.
3. The infant's paternal grandmother is unknown, the father being unknown; but, in any circumstance, I am told, it is the maternal, not the paternal grandmother who attends the presentation rite.
4. The other members are Wana's father and Wana's three-year-old daughter.
5. Another informant, describing the presentation rite in general, asserted that the grandmother would not say any prayer.
6. Also translated "grow strong." Another informant insisted that this word should be translated "to know about it."
7. In other connections her name was always given as Getsitsa.
8. In Pueblo ceremonials sacrosanct things are commonly breathed upon, and impersonators of the gods, at Zuñi at least, breathe upon the layman. According to Stevenson, the Sia infant is breathed on. ("The Sia," p. 141.)
9. An unfamiliar word. The *cheani* have a peculiar vocabulary.
10. *Cp.* Parsons, E.C.:"Zuñi Death Beliefs and Practices."—*American Anthropologist.* XVIII, (1916), 246.
11. According to other informants names are suggested by the medicine-man, but not at the presentation rite. (*Cp.* "The Sia," p. 141.)
12. The board was painted turquoise.
13. Nor should water lying in the road be drunk. It would cause tuberculosis—"there are so many travellers in a road."
14. Parsons, E.C.:"Zuñi Conception and Pregnancy Beliefs."— *Proc. XIX, International Congress of Americanists,* pp. 382-3. Washington, 1917.
15. Cp. "The Sia," p. 141.

Zuni women and children
reluctantly photographed,
ca. 1920. Courtesy of the
Museum of New Mexico,
Negative no. 145948.

Mothers and Children at Zuñi, New Mexico

In Zuñi girls are more desirable than boys, and it is with reluctance that a man of the household will be summoned to help at child-birth—except in an emergency the men are sent out of the house[1]—for the presence of a man will turn the unborn girl into a boy. A nap during labour likewise results in a change of sex, making of the boy, a girl, or of the girl, a boy. Movement of the foetus on the right side is a sign of a girl, on the left side, of a boy. Slight pains indicate that a girl is to be born, and the women present will say to the expectant mother, "Don't sleep or you will have a boy."

During labour a raw bean may be swallowed—just as it slips down with ease the delivery will be easy.[2] The labour will be hard if, during her pregnancy, the woman has been subject to much cold —the waters in her freeze and "hold the baby back." While the assistant is massaging the abdomen she will feel the top of her patient's head—it will get hot when the time of delivery is at hand. When the placenta is retarded, the woman will be slapped on the lower part of the back with a man's moccasin[3]—"a man walks fast about his fields."[4]

At once after the birth, a boy is sprinkled on the penis with cold water that the parts may be small, and a girl has placed over the vulva a gourd cup, that the parts may be large. These requirements in physical proportion are distinctively feminine, as men will say to women, "Why do you want us small and yourselves large?" After the baby's hot cedar bath he or she will be rubbed all over with ashes to keep the body depilous for life. Hair on body or face is disliked. Not infrequently when a man is talking to you he will be tweaking out hairs from his face with the square inch of metal tweezers he carries about for that service.

During eight days[5] the mother lies in on a three-inch bed of hot sand, quilt or blanket over the sand. A like bed is made for the baby. A box is placed back of his head to hold the cover off his face. Before placing the box it is rapped smartly on the ground, rapped north, west, south, and east, that thereafter the child may be inattentive to noises—an instance of the inoculative magic to which the Zuñi are much addicted.[6] The head of the baby is to the west.[7] It is important for the mother to lie on her stomach; should she lie on her back the milk would sink back into her body. It is important, too, for her to keep drinking hot cedar brew, "that all the blood will come out," and none be left "to make another baby." A baby thus made

would be small and sickly. For the same reason there is a rule or dis-
inclination against having intercourse until the flow has ceased.

The mother's hot drinks have been prepared by the baby's paternal
grandmother, his wowa. She, too, has kept the sand-bed hot, as well as
the stone pressed to the mother's abdomen, and she has given the baby
a daily bath. In return for these services *an wowa* will receive meat and
bread and *he'paluke*, wheat meal cooked in corn husk. On the morning
of the eighth day, before sunrise, *an wowa* comes to take mother and child
outdoors to present the child to the sun. The grandmother sprinkles meal
on the ground and prays:—

> *Yatokya lithl hon yam teapkunan illikwaikya to' onnayaky'ana*
> Sun here we your baby (prayer word) take out you road finished
> *utenananichiaky'ana.*
> good things get.

After this rite, after the baby has flown out like a fledgling from its nest,
people say, the baby is put for the first time on his board cradle. In this
cradle, near where the heart of the baby would be, a little hole is made and
filled with piñon gum, and a bit of turquoise inlaid.[8] This is to give a heart
to the cradle, "to make it come alive" (*temmeikyenaiya*=board, give heart),
and to preclude it from bringing any harm to its tenant.[9] If a baby dies, its
cradle is burned;[10] were it used for another child, the child would die.

A baby runs great risk if it is left in a room alone. Some family ghost
whose heart is in the house will return and hold the baby, and in four days
the baby will die. I was told the story of just such an occurrence. Recently
a woman who had left her baby alone re-entered the room, and the baby
was nowhere to be seen. She searched everywhere in vain. She went to
inquire of neighbours. On her return she found the baby where she had
left it. In four days the baby died. If a baby has to be left alone, an ear
of corn, the kind of ear which is flattened and quasi-branching at the tip,[11]
should be left alongside.

If the baby has a rash, it is due to the fact that before his birth his
mother tested the heat of her own oven by sprinkling bran in it. To cure
the rash, the mother will soak some bran in water and rub it over the baby.
Sores on a baby may be due to his mother stepping before his birth on
an anthill. To cure *halonaiye* (ants on body), the mother will carry the
child four times across an anthill—as usual in Zuñi thought, like cures like.
But if this treatment fail, a medicine-man from the Ant Society will be
invited to the child's home. There for four nights he will set up a ground
altar and engage in the rite of brushing the ants out of the patient's body
into the circle of meal on the altar. In one case described to me the brush
(*pepe*) was seen to be full of pebbles and ants, and the baby did indeed
recover.

In another instance I heard of, the baby's sores looked like the spots of paint on the mask his mother in her pregnancy had seen worn by his father. To cure the baby they put paint on it, and at the same time on the mask. Disfigurement in the baby may be caused before his birth by his father taking part in a masked dance. The mask is said to be copied (*teliyasheye*) in the baby. Then the father will put on his mask and dance, and sweat from his body will be rubbed on the baby.[12] Sweat from a horse will be rubbed on a baby if it cries as if in pain, for the pain may have been caused by the father beating his horses. If the baby cries a great deal, it is because his father sang a great deal before he was born, and for such crying there is no remedy. One day we had for dinner an unexpected mutton stew. "A man sent me a sheep which he said he owed me," explained our hostess. "I had forgotten about it. Last summer his baby was very sick, and they thought it might be because the father[13] had got drunk before the baby was born. So they wanted to rub some whiskey on the baby. I happened to have a bottle of Virginia Dare wine and I gave it to them." The baby had died.[14]

This baby, like others, died unnamed. Not until a child is creeping about does it get a name. They put off the naming until there is comparative certainty of living, for should a baby have a name and die, they would recall the name, and "it would make them feel worse." The child will be named by some senior in the family—named, perhaps, for a relative long since dead. They would not give the name of a living person or of one recently dead about whom "they still feel bad." In this instance, as in others, it is plain that after the set mourning of four days the dead are put out of mind as thoroughly as possible.

The baby that has been born at full moon has a good prospect of health and long life; born on the new moon or on the waning moon his prospects are poor. The time for initiation into the secret societies is set in January and February at the full moons, because being initiated is like being born—a point of view familiar in other communities.

If a woman has had a hard time in raising her children, she will ask a *shiwanni* (so-called rain priest) to name a child. The *shiwanni* (in case of a boy a man *shiwanni*, in case of a girl a woman *shiwanni*) will come to the child's house and put a little water on the child's forehead. The rite is referred to as *mito'u*, a term for putting anything on the forehead. There can be little doubt that this rite has been borrowed from the *tutatsi*, the Catholic priest, by the *ashiwanni*.[15] In the characteristically Pueblo rite of washing, the whole head is washed. According to an aged woman informant, people stopped going to the church for baptism some decades ago. Once a woman had lain down in the church contrary to the order of the bow-priests, those strict guardians of the proprieties even when borrowed, and nursed her baby. Four days later mother and baby died. This so frightened the people that they stopped going to church.

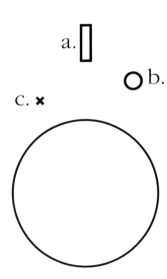

Diagram:
Altar of Medicine-Man of Ant Society.
a = mi'li, *corn ear fetich;*
b = *medicine bowl into which* c *is dropped and out of which all present are given a drink at close of the ceremony;*
c = aklashi, *old stone, fetich which looked into reveals cause of sickness;*
d = *circle of meal into which ants are brushed and out of which they will not move.*

An unfortunate mother has still other resources. She will ask to have the *santu* brought out, *i.e.*, transferred from the inner room in the house of its sacristan to the front room, and candles will be lit and prayers said. The woman will *santu yechu*—breathe in from the *santu, i.e.*, she will draw a breath four times from her own clasped hands while feeling she is acquiring virtue from the saint. *Yechu* is a rite of virtue getting or fortune getting practised in connection with any fetich or object possessed of fetichistic quality.

Again, to ensure success with the coming child a woman may be given a *wiha* (baby) or doll made up as a *koko* or masked impersonation. She will receive it from a *koko* during a dance.[16] After the birth of the child the *wiha* is referred to as the "heart" of the child, and for neither love nor money will the mother part with this *wiha*.[17] It is a kind of life token.[18] Were it disposed of, "the child it had brought would die."

Analogously, a woman who has received prayer-sticks from a *shiwanni* to plant at the phallic shrine on *towa yallene*[19] and who thereby gets a child will show attentions to the given *shiwanni* lest her child die. I heard of one such mother who was accustomed to bring food to the *ashiwanni* of the South during their eight-day summer retreat to call the rain. As if she were a member of a *shiwanni* household, during the retreat this woman devotee did not trade. In another case I heard of, because the woman failed to go on with her gifts to the *ashiwanni*, to whose altar in the winter solstice ceremonial she had brought the clay image of a baby, she did not succeed in getting a child.

Another success bringing method is to invite to be present at the birth a woman who has had many children and lost none.[20] She will be the first to pick up the new-born, and she will blow into his mouth (*pu'ana*). In case of a boy, her husband or some man in her house[21] will become the boy's initiator or ceremonial father in the *kotikyanne* or god society into which all the boys are initiated.[22] Ordinarily a boy's father chooses a man in the household of his *kuku*, his paternal aunt, to become his son's ceremonial father.[23]

The development of the child is promoted in several particulars. That he may keep well and walk early, hairs from a deer are burned and the baby held over the smoke—deer are never sick, and rapid is their gait. Their hearing, too, is acute, so discharge from a deer's ear may be put into the baby's ear. That he may teeth quickly, his gums are rubbed by one who has been bitten by a snake. The snake-bitten will also rub the gums if, after the teeth have erupted, the child tries to bite everything. "Snakes want to bite"—once more inoculative magic.

That a child may talk well and with tongues, the tongue of a snared mocking-bird may be cut out and held to the baby to lick. The bird will then be released in order that, as it regains its tongue and "talks," the child

Zuni children photographed by Matilda Coxe Stevenson, 1891-1896. Note shadow of photographer in picture. Courtesy of the Museum of New Mexico, Neg. no. 82371.

will talk. To the brother of my informant mocking-bird tongue had been thus applied, and to-day the youth speaks, in addition to his native language, Keresan, English, and Spanish.

To make a child's hair grow long and thick, his grandfather or uncle may puff the smoke of native tobacco on his head.[24] Hair cuttings are burned. Were they thrown out, the winds would scatter the hairs and with them the life and fortune of their producer.[25] Besides, witches work ill through air. At the *koko awia* (*shalako*) ceremonial, when many Navajo guests are at hand, hair brushes are scrupulously hidden away. If a baby keeps his fists tight, they are not prised open to wash, because the dirt he holds is said to be good life and good fortune; the baby who keeps his palms open will be without fortune.

The first time a baby is taken out at night, embers moistened with water are rubbed over his heart that he may not be afraid in the dark. Similarly, dampened embers are rubbed over a child's heart when he wakes up from a nightmare, and water with embers in it is given to him to drink. The first time a baby is taken any distance from home his mother would turn her head soon after she had left the house and, as if the baby were not in her arms but behind in the road, she would call out, "Come, you are the last behind there, but come, don't cry." Thereafter, on leaving home, the baby will not cry.[26] The first time a member of the household puts the baby on her back to carry him the baby is whipped. In the novel position he is whipped four times, whipped on his buttocks with a bit of yucca. This measure will keep the baby from crying thereafter on being carried. My informant remembered how her mother had said to her when she first picked up a baby sister to carry on her back. "Wait, stand still," and had gone to get the yucca switch.

In washing a baby's clothes, much care is taken not to drop any garment—the child would have a bad fall. For this reason the clothes would not be hung on a line.

When a drooling baby coughs, his grandmother (*an wowa*)[27] is said to be saving something to give him; she is said to be talking about him when he sneezes.[28]

Notes

Originally published in *Man*, no. 86, November 1919, pp. 168-73. The original footnote symbols have been converted to numerals and numbered consecutively as endnotes.

1. Parsons, E. C.:"Zuñi Conception and Pregnancy Beliefs," p. 380. *Proc. 19th Inter. Congress of Americanists,* Washington, D.C., 1915. The phallic shrine for girl babies mentioned in this account is called *tepokwa* (vulva). The stone within, *ashon,* is not only scraped for would-be mothers to drink, but it is touched by one who wants a wife.
2. This practice appears to be unknown at Laguna. There, at the onset of labour, a midwife will put a badger claw into the woman's belt. The motive was obscure to my informant, but I suspect it is because the badger is "good at digging his way out," a reason I have heard advanced by Keresans for badger service in other ceremonial connections. (*Cp.* "Franciscan Fathers," *An Ethnologic Dictionary of the Navaho Language,* p. 413, St. Michael's, Arizona, 1910.) On the other hand, the badger may be thought to have some responsibility for labour pains, and therefore to be good medicine against them.
3. There is the same practice at Laguna. Again, at Laguna, in case of retardation, the tip of a deer's horn may be ground fine, mixed with water and drunk—the deer's horn is strong, it pulls asunder. The placenta is sacred (*tsityu*), and so it is not thrown out indifferently, but buried near the river, where it will be washed away, the customary disposal of sacrosanct discards. Were it treated less carefully, ill-health would befall the woman. The cord is buried under the house floor, near the grinding stones, in case of a girl, in the middle of a field, in case of a boy, with the intent to attract the child either to grinding or to field work. At Zuñi something which is called *suuke* (certain cave dwelling bogeys) *shonshi* (nail, claw), is found by a man of the household and applied to the severed cord to make it heal quickly.
4. Incidentally I may note that the dye will come off men's moccasins if a pregnant woman sees them in the making. In like circumstances black spots will come out on bowls in firing.
5. The customary period in different families is not uniform. A confinement of four days, I was once told, was copied from the Navajo. The ceremonial confinement of the *chakwena okya* (woman), a masked impersonation, is eight days. "We do as the *chakwena okya*," said one informant, "to save our babies."
6. *Cp.* Parsons, E. C.:"Zuñi Inoculative Magic"—*Science,* N.S., XLIV (1916), pp. 469-70. For a like point of view in a Plains tribe, *see* Kroeber, A. L., "The Arapaho"—*Bull. Amer. Mus. Nat. Hist.,* XVIII (1907), p. 451.
7. The position of the dead is head to the east, and none would think of sleeping in that position.
8. In one cradle I have seen there were two turquoise insets, one on either side of the neck rest of the cradle. This cradle had been made by the father's people, since, contrary to the more common usage, the mother was living with them.
9. Turquoise is laid in the foundations of a new house, and, I surmise, from much the same point of view. At Laguna to-day turquoise is not set into the cradle, but the reference to turquoise in the lullaby printed in MAN, 1919, **18**, suggests that turquoise was once used as at Zuñi, or among the Navaho. (*An Ethnologic Dictionary of the Navaho Language,* p. 470.) Wood struck by lightning should be used for the cradle that the baby may grow. Lightning is *kokimuni*, possessed of supernatural powers. A little bag containing corn pollen and four grains of corn, the heart of the child, is tied to the heart side, *i.e.,* left side of the board cradle. The four grains have been taken from the ear of corn that has lain alongside the infant the first four days of his life. The rest of the

corn is planted that the child may grow with the corn. In curing, the patient's heart is also represented by, or rather identified with, four grains of corn.

10. Among the Apache a dead baby is encradled, and baby and cradle are hung on a tree. Personal communication from Dr. P. E. Goddard. (*Cp. An Ethnologic Dictionary of the Navaho Language*, p. 472.)

11. The ear of corn which splits in two toward the top (*mi' kyapana*, corn, flat) is thought of as a mother and child. It is kept in the corn store room, in some cases together with a lump of salt (*makyapana,*). When salt is dug from the Salt Lake the hole soon fills up. The lump of salt is kept in the corn store, so that whatever corn is removed will be made good. For like reason a lump is kept at the bottom of the bread bowl. A lump of salt may also be left alongside the baby.

12. For analogous explanations of deformity, *see Zuñi Conception and Pregnancy Beliefs* pp. 382-3.

13. The mother as well as the father may have been the cause of sickness. Both parents will try out remedies. A successful remedy is proof of the cause of the sickness.

14. In this household there had been three deaths within a few months, two girl babies and a thirteen-year-old girl. Several causes were considered. A few months before there had been a lunar eclipse—"the moon died"—and many deaths among females had followed. A few years before, the house had been one of the houses of entertainment during the *koko awia* ceremonial. It was suggested that one of the god impersonations might have been a witch. Witch malignities of more recent date were also considered. A corn-ear fetich (*mi' le*) hanging up in its bag had fallen and broken a ceremonial bowl below. This was interpreted as an omen (*teliuna*) of the misfortunes that followed.

15. A Catholic baptismal rite is used in curing a child with dysentery among the Pima. (Russell, F.:"The Pima Indians," pp. 266-7, xxvi (1905), *Ann. Rep. Bur. Amer. Ethnol.*

16. Father Dumarest describes a like practice in connection with would-be mothers among the Keresans of Cochiti. (MS. to be published as a Memoir of the American Anthropological Association in 1919). *Cp.* to the ear of corn given to a would-be mother by the *chakwa*n *okya.* (Parsons, E. C.:"Notes on Zuñi," II, 179—*Mem. Amer. Anthr. Assoc.,* Vol. IV, No. 4, 1917).

17. *Wiwe* given to the children themselves by the *koko* are less precious. They are of the same type as the *auwak* of Laguna, the female, boardlike, the male, a rounded block. *See* "Mothers and Children at Laguna, New Mexico."

18. The life token representation appears again in the *mi' li,* the feather-girt ear of corn acquired by members of the curing orders. "A person lives as long as his *mi' li* wants him to live," and at death the *mi' li* is buried, the corn planted, and the feathers made into a prayer stick.

19. *Zuñi Conception and Pregnancy Beliefs,* p. 379.

20. The same practice is followed at Laguna.

21. In one case of which I heard, it was her son-in-law. Her daughter took the child to be baptized by the *tutatsi* in the house of the *santu, i.e.,* became his godmother—as interesting an instance of how Zuñi pattern imposes itself upon foreign custom as any I know, a native fertility birth practice combining with a Catholic rite.

22. The boys are taken in at the quadrennial initiation between the years of six and ten. The bow-priests oppose the complete initiation of the very young because of the ceremonial improprieties they may commit. Once a little boy dancer came out with his mask raised from his face, and, as usual in case of ceremonial mishaps, all the people had to be cleansed by whipping by the *sayathlia,* exorcising masks.

23. This practice is in accordance with the general Zuñi theory that ceremonial functions devolve upon the father's people. Stevenson has mistaken the particular practice, or as much of it as she was told about, I surmise, for the general practice.

24. At Laguna willow twigs are twisted up and put in the water to wash the hair, that the hair may be long like the willows.

25. *Cp.* "Mothers and Children at Laguna, New Mexico," MAN, 1919, **18**.

26. Is this practice Spanish? Curiously enough the same practice is followed by the negroes of the Sea Islands of South Carolina.

27. *Cp.* Parsons, E. C.:"Notes on Ceremonialism at Laguna." To be published in Vol. XIX, of *Papers of the American Museum of Natural History.* The substitution at Zuñi of the baby's grandmother for mother *iyetik,* the earth supernatural of Laguna, is of interest. The latter, *awitelin tsita,* earth mother as she is called at Zuñi, has a much more esoteric or distant position at Zuñi than at Laguna.

28. Similarly, if an adult sneezes, someone is talking about him. If he sneezes at night, it is a ghost talking about him. "Last night my husband sneezed," said my informant, "he thought it was a dead sweetheart talking, and he said to her, 'Wait until that little mouse gets a long tail, then I will go to see you.' "

Waiyautitsa of Zuñi, New Mexico

Only twice through my association with Pueblo Indians has it occurred to me to be a feminist. The first time was at Cochiti when late at night my tired and sleepy Indian hostess grumbled in the soft tones no Pueblo woman ever loses, grumbled because she had to sit up for the young husband who was spending the evening at the club, *i.e.*, taking part in a ceremonial at the estufa. "I'll have to get him something to eat," she said, "no man here would ever cook for himself at home. They say if they did, they would lose their sense of the trail." Rationalization of habit or desire is not confined to the peoples of western civilization.

The second time I remembered I was a feminist was when the editor of a certain journal asked me to write an article on Zuñi women. Are the women of a community still thought of, I queried, even in scientific or pseudo-scientific circles, as a separable class? If so, there is nothing for us but to keep on with the categories of feminist and anti-feminist, tiresome though they become.

Well, the article was written, but it was not published because it contained a reference to the lack of prostitution at Zuñi. Recognition of the subject was considered unsuitable for boy and girl readers; it was deemed better for them to have a partial survey of the facts of life than to see life whole, even at Zuñi. Nor was life at Zuñi to suggest inquiry into life at home.

But writing the article served at least one purpose. It focused attention upon the differentiation of the sexes at Zuñi and resulted in an analysis which contributed to the understanding of a considerable portion of Zuñi habits of mind and of culture. To get the survey which leads to the analysis, let us follow the life of a baby girl we shall call Waiyautitsa, a girl's name, for sex generally appears in Zuñi personal names. Sex appears somewhat in speech too. Waiyautitsa in learning to talk will make use of expressions, particularly exclamations, peculiar to women. Recently Dr. Kroeber, in giving us a list of the first words used by a Zuñi child, a boy, noted the comparatively large number of kinship terms in his vocabulary. The kinship terms of our imaginary little girl would be somehwat different from a boy's. He calls a younger sister *ikina*; a younger brother, *suw;* she calls either *hani*, meaning merely the younger. And, as the Zuñi system of kinship terms is what is called classificatory, cousins having the same terms as brother and sister, Waiyautitsa has even fewer words than her brother to express cousinship.

Facing Page:

Zuni girl carrying baby, ca. 1900. A Keystone View Co. stereogram. Courtesy of the Museum of New Mexico, Negative no. 89326.

When Waiyautitsa is three or four years old she may be recognized as a girl not merely from her speech, but from her dress, from her cotton slip; at this age little boys wear trousers. But not for another three or four years, perhaps longer, will Waiyautitsa wear over her cotton slip the characteristic Pueblo woman's dress,—the black blanket dress fastened on the left shoulder and under the right arm and hence called in Zuñi *watone*, meaning "across," the broad belt woven of white, green and red cotton, the store-bought kerchief or square of silk (*pitone*) which, fastened in front, hangs across shoulders and back, and the small foot, thick leg moccasins which cover ankle and calf in an envelope of fold upon fold of buckskin. Before Waiyautitsa is eight or even six she may, however, when she goes out, cover her head and body with a black blanket or with the gay colored "shawl" similarly worn. And I have seen very little girls indeed wearing moccasins or the footless black stockings Zuñi women also wear, or "dressing up" in a *pitone*, that purely ornamental article of dress without which no Zuñi woman would venture outdoors. Without her *pitone* she would feel naked, she says, and any man would be at liberty to speak disrespectfully to her. When Waiyautitsa is about five, her hair, before this worn, like the boys, in a short cut, is let grow into a little tail on the nape of her neck. In course of time her pigtail will be turned up and tied with a "hair belt" of white, green and red cloth. From ear to ear her front hair will be banged to the end of her nose, the bang drawn sidewise above the forehead except at such times in ceremonials when it is let fall forward to conceal the upper part of the face.

This hair arrangement serves in ceremonials as a kind of mask. A mask proper, that *quasi* fetich which has so important a place in Pueblo ceremonialism, Waiyautitsa will in all probability never wear. Unlike her brother, Waiyautitsa will not be initiated in childhood into the *kotikyane* or god society, and consequently she will not join one of the six *kiwitsiwe* or sacred club-houses or estufas which supply personators for the masked "dancers." Not that female personages do not figure in these ceremonials, but as was the rule on the Elizabethan stage women are impersonated by men.

To this exclusion of girls from the *kotikyane* and from participating in the masked "dances" there are, we should note, a few exceptions. To-day three women belong to the *kotikyane*. They were taken into it not in childhood, but in later life and, it is said, for one of the same reasons women as well as men are taken into the other fraternities or societies of Zuñi. Cured by ceremonial whipping of the bad effects of nightmare or of some other ailment, they were "given" to the *kiwitsine* credited through one of its members with the cure. Of the three women members only one is said to dance, and she is accounted mannish, *katsotse*, girl-man, a tomboy.

Waiyautitsa will not be initiated, it is not very likely, into the *kotikyane*, but she is quite likely to be initiated into another society,—into the Great Fire or Little Fire or Bed Bug or Ant or Wood society, into any one of the thirteen Zuñi societies except three, the bow priesthood or society of warriors, of warriors who have taken a scalp, or the Hunter Society or the Cactus Society, a society that cures arrow or gun-shot wounds. As women do not hunt or go to war, from membership in these groups they are excluded or, better say, precluded. As we shall see later, affiliation by sex is in ceremonial affairs along the lines of customary occupation.

If Waiyautitsa falls sick and is cured by a medicine-man of the medicine order of a society she must be "given" either to the family of the medicine man or to his society. Initiated she may not be, however, for a long time afterwards, perhaps for years. Initiations take place in the winter when school is in session, the school either of the Indian Bureau or of the Dutch Reformed Church, and for that reason, it is said, initiations may be postponed until past school age. Despite the schools, I may say, I have met but two Zuñi women who speak English with any fluency. One woman is a member of the Snake-Medicine Society, into which she was initiated after convalescence from measles, a decimating disease at Zuñi, to be accounted for only through witchcraft. The other woman was accounted the solitary convert of the Dutch Reform Church Mission in Zuñi until six or seven years ago she joined the Wood society because as a child she had been cured by them of smallpox.

After initiation, the women, like the men of a society, offer feather-sticks each moon, observing continence for four days thereafter, and they join in the four-day retreat in the ceremonial house of the society preliminary to an initiation. Unlike the men, however, the women do not spend the entire night, only the evening, in the society house, and, while there, they are listeners rather than narrators of the inexhaustible folk tales that are wont to be told at society gatherings. Men are the custodians of the lore, secular as well as esoteric, of the tribe, just as men and not women are the musicians. The men are devoted singers, singing as they dance or singing as a choir for dancers, and singing as they go to or from work in the fields or as they drive their horses to water in the river or to the corrals on the edges of the town. Even grinding songs are sung on ceremonial occasions by men.

In the public appearances of the society, the women members figure but little. Societies supply choirs and drummers and ceremonial road openers or leaders to the masked dancers and, during the great *koko awia* (god coming) or *shalako* ceremonial, to various groups of sacred personages. I have seen several "dances" in Zuñi and one celebration of *koko awia*, and I have seen but one woman officiate in public. As a daughter of the house which was entertaining the *koyemshi* or sacred clowns she was in attendance upon that group in the *koko awia* or Advent, so to speak, of 1915.

If Waiyautitsa belongs to a society, she will offer or plant the befeathered prayer-sticks, which are so conspicuous a feature of Pueblo religion, but, being a woman, Waiyautitsa will not cut or dress the sticks. She will only grind the pigments and, perhaps, paint the sticks. Nor as a woman would she offer the sticks on certain other ceremonial occasions when the men offer them. Once a year, however, at the winter solstice ceremonial on which so much of Zuñi ritual pivots, Waiyautitsa will be expected, even in infancy, to plant, planting for the "old ones," *i.e.*, the ancestors and for the Moon, but not, like the men, for the Sun or, unless a member of the *kotikyane*, for the ancestral gods, the *koko*.

At the conclusion of the winter solstice ceremonial, when certain sacred figures called *kwelele* go from house to house, the women carry embers around the walls of the house and throw them out on the *kwelele*. It is a rite of *shuwaha*, cleansing, exorcism. There are a number of other little rites peculiar to the women in Zuñi ceremonialism. Through them, and through a number of rites they share with the men, through provisions for supplying food in the *kiwitsine* to the sacred personators or for entertaining them at home or making them presents, women have an integral part in Zuñi ceremonialism. In what we may call the ceremonial management, however, they appear to have little or no part.

Even when women are initiated into the *kotikyane*, or are associated with the *ashiwanni* or rain priests, their functions seem to be primarily of an economic or housekeeping order. The women members of the rain priesthoods have to offer food every day to the fetiches of these sacerdotal groups—to stones carved and uncarved and to cotton wrapped lengths of cane filled with "the seeds the people live by." For the seed fetiches to be in any way disturbed in the houses to which they are attached involves great danger to the people and on a woman in the house, the woman member of the priesthood, falls the responsibility of guardianship or shelter. But even these positions of trust are no longer held by women—there are, according to Dr. Kroeber, only six women *ashiwanni* among the fifteen priesthoods. The woman's position among the paramount priesthood, the rain priesthood of the North, has been vacant now for many years—no suitable woman being willing, they say, to run the risks or be under the taboos of office. Aside from this position of woman *shiwanni*, women count for little or nothing in the theocracy of Zuñi. They were and are associated with the men priests to do the work pertinent to women. In the case of the Zuñi pantheon or its masked impersonations, the association is needed to satisfy or carry out, so to speak, Zuñi standards or concepts of conjugality. The couple rather than the individual is the Zuñi unit. Sometimes, in ceremony or in myth, the couple may consist of two males.

Facing Page:

"Zuñi Girls at the River," 1903. Photograph by Edward S. Curtis. Courtesy of the Museum of New Mexico, Negative no. 76957.

There is one masked couple I have noted in particular at Zuñi, the *atoshle.* Two or three times during the winter our little Waiyautitsa together with other girls and very little boys may expect to be frightened by the *atoshle,* the disciplinary masks who serve as bugaboos to children as well as a kind of sergeant-at-arms, the male *atoshle* at least, for adults. If the children meet the old man and his old woman in the street, they run away helter skelter. If the dreadful couple visits a child indoors, sent for perhaps by a parent, the child is indeed badly frightened. I suppose that Waiyautitsa is six or seven years old when one day, as an incident of some dance, the *atoshle* "come out" and come to her house. The old woman *atoshle* carries a deep basket on her back in which to carry off naughty children and in her hand a crook to catch them by the ankle. With the crook she pulls Waiyautitsa over to the grinding stones in the corner of the room, telling her that now she is getting old enough to help her mother about the house, to look after the baby and, before so very long, to grind. She must mind her mother and be a good girl. I once saw a little girl so terrified by such admonition—this time by the old man *atoshle,* the old woman not being along—that she began to whimper, hiding her head in her mother's lap until the *atoshle* was sprinkled with the sacred meal and left the house to perform elsewhere his role of parents' assistant.

Whether from fear, from supernatural fear or fear of being talked about as any Zuñi woman who rests or idles is talked about, or whether from example, more from the latter no doubt than from the former, Waiyautitsa is certainly a "good girl," a gentle little creature, and very docile. Through imitating her industrious mother or aunt or her even more industrious grandmother or great-aunt, she learns to do all the household tasks of women. She learns to grind the corn on the stone *metate*—that back-hardening labor of the Pueblo woman—and to pre-pare and cook the meal in a number of ways in an outside oven or on the American stove or on the flat slab on which *hewe* or wafer bread is spread. For the ever cheery family meal she sets out the coffee-pot, the *hewe* or *tortilla,* and the bowls of chile and of mutton stew on the earthen floor she is forever sweeping up with her little home-made brush or with an American broom. (A Zuñi house is kept very clean and amazingly neat and orderly.)

And Waiyautitsa becomes very thrifty—not only naturally but su-pernaturally. She will not sell corn out of the house without keeping back a few grains in order that the corn may return—in Zuñi thought the whole follows a part. And she will keep a lump of salt in the corn store room and another in the bread bowl—when salt is dug out, the hole soon refills, and this virtue of replacing itself the salt is expected to impart to the corn. There are other respects, too, in which Waiyautitsa will learn how to facilitate the economy. She will sprinkle the melon seeds for planting with sweetened water—melons should be sweet. Seed wheat she will sprinkle with a white clay to make the crop white, and with a plant called ko'wa so that wheat dough will pull well. Seed corn will be sprinkled with water that the crop may be well rained on.

From some kinswoman who is a specially good potter Waiyautitsa may have learned to coil and paint and fire the bowls as well as the cook pots and water jars the household needs. She fetches in wood from the wood-pile and now and again she may be seen chopping the pine or cedar logs the men of the household have brought in on donkey or in wagon. She fetches water from one of the modern wells of the town, carrying it in a jar on her head and walking in the slow and springless gait always characteristic of Pueblo women. That gait, let me say, so ponderous and so different from the gait of the men, is one of the puzzling things about Pueblo women. Is it perhaps the result of their incessant industry, a kind of unconscious self-protective device against "speeding up"?

Waiyautitsa will learn to work outdoors as well as in. She will help her mother in keeping one of the small gardens near the town—the men cultivate the outlying fields of corn and wheat (and the men and boys herd the sheep which make the Zuñi prosperous), and Waiyautitsa will help her household thresh their wheat crop, in the morning preparing dinner for the workers, for relatives from other households as well as from her own, in the afternoon joining the threshers as the men drive horses or mules around the circular threshing floor and the women and girls pitchfork the wheat and brush away the chaff and winnow the grain in baskets. Waiyautitsa will also learn to make adobe blocks and to plaster with her bare hand or with a rabbit-skin glove the adobe walls of her mother's house, inside and out. Pueblo men are the carpenters of a house, but the women are always the plasterers, and Waiyautitsa will have to be a very old womn indeed to think she is too old to plaster. On my last visit to Zuñi I saw a woman seventy or not much under spending part of an afternoon on her knees plastering the chinks of a door newly cut between two rooms.

The house she plasters belongs or will in time belong to Waiyautitsa. Zuñi women own their houses and their gardens or, perhaps it is better to say, gardens and houses belong to the family through the women. At marriage a girl does not leave home; her husband joins her household. He stays in it, too, only as long as he is welcome. If he is lazy, if he fails to bring in wood, if he fails to contribute the produce of his fields, or if some one else for some other reason is preferred, his wife expects him to leave her household. He does not wait to be told twice. "The Zuñi separate whenever they quarrel or get tired of each other," a critical Acoma moralist once said to me. The monogamy of Zuñi is, to be sure, rather brittle. In separation the children stay with the mother.

Children belong to their mother's clan. They have affiliations, however, as we shall see, with the clan of their father. If the mother of Waiyautitsa is a Badger, let us say, and her father a Turkey, Waiyautitsa will be a Badger and "the child of the Turkey." She can not marry a Turkey clansman nor, of course, a Badger. Did she show any partiality for a clansman, an almost incredible thing, she would be told she was just like a dog or a burro.

These exogamous restrictions aside and the like restrictions that may arise in special ways between the household of Waiyautitsa and other households, Waiyautitsa would be given, I am told, freedom of choice in marrying. Even if her household did not like her man, and her parents had told her not "to talk to" him, Zuñi for courting, she and he could go to live with some kinswoman. No one, related or unrelated, would refuse to take them in. In Zuñi nobody may be turned from the door. Nor would a girl whose child was the offspring of a chance encounter be turned out by her people or slighted. The illegitimate child is not discriminated against at Zuñi.

Casual relationships occur at Zuñi, but they are not commercialized, there is no prostitution. Nor is there any life-long celibacy. As for courtship, how there can be any, at least before intimacy either in the more transient or more permanent forms of mating, is a puzzle—the separation outside of the household of boys and girls of various ages is so thorough. "But what if a little girl wanted to play with boys?" I once asked. "They would laugh at her and say she was too crazy about boys." "Crazy" at Zuñi, as quite generally among Indians, means passionate. (Girls at Zuñi are warned away from ceremonial trespass by the threat of becoming "crazy.")

The young men and the girls do, to be sure, have non-ceremonial dances together, and in preparing for them there may be opportunities for personal acquaintance. The dance itself seems too formal for such opportunities. I saw one of these dances not long ago. It was a Comanche dance. There were a choir of about a dozen youths including the drummer, four girl dancers heavily beringed and benecklaced, the pattern of whose dance, two by two or in line, was very regular, and a youth who executed in front of them or around them an animated and very beautiful *pas seul.* After dancing outside in the plaza, they all went into "the saints house" to dance for her "because they like her"—a survival no doubt of the custom of dancing in the Catholic church observed by the Indians in Mexico and not long since quite generally in New Mexico. During this same visit to Zuñi, I may say, I also saw one late afternoon, a time for fetching water, a young man take a girl rather brusquely by the arm and try to speak to her. She averted her head and passed on, another girl only a few steps ahead of her and another not far behind. It was the briefest

*Zuni women baking
bread for a feast, ca.
1891. Photographed by
Matilda Coxe Stevenson.
Courtesy of the Museum
of New Mexico, Negative
no. 82363.*

of encounters and far from private, but it left me no longer quite as sceptical as I had been on being told that at this twilight hour, at least, the girls and the young men do meet. And after "two or four" meetings at the well a girl may agree to marry or, in Zuñi phrase, to have a man.

Well, Waiyautitsa has in one way or another, we shall have to suppose, met her young man and agreed that he is to join her household. At first, for a few days, he will stay in the common room, in the room where all sleep (sleeping and dressing, let me say, with the utmost modesty), he will stay only at night, leaving before dawn, "staying still" his shyness is called. Then he will begin to eat his meals with the household. There is, you see, no wedding ceremonial and a man slips as easily as he can into the life of his wife's household. The Ashiwi, as the people call themselves, take no pleasure in disconcerting one another— ceremonially, at least—nor does the priesthood aim to direct domestic events.

Waiyautitsa will pay a formal visit on her bridegroom's people, taking his mother a basket of corn meal. To Waiyautitsa herself her young man will have given a present of cloth for a dress or a buckskin for the moccasins he will make for her. Hides are a product of the chase, of cattle raising (cowhide is used to sole moccasins), or of trade, men's occupations, and so moccasins of both women and men are made by men. Women make their own dresses, although, formerly, before weaving went out of fashion at Zuñi, it is likely that men were the weavers, just as they are to-day among the Hopi from whom the men of Zuñi get cloth for their ceremonial kilts and blankets and for the dresses of the women. Even to-day at Zuñi men may make up their own garments from store bought goods and it is not unusual to see a man sitting to a sewing-machine.

A man may use cloth or thread for other than economic reasons. In case a girl jilts him he will catch her out some night and take a bit from her belt to fasten to a tree on a windy mesa top. As the wind wears away the thread, the woman will sicken and perhaps in two or three years die.[1] A woman who is deserted may take soil from the man's footprints and put it where she sleeps. At night he will think of her and come back—"even if the other woman is better looking." Apprehensive of desertion a woman may put a lock of hair from the man in her house wall or, the better to attach him to her, she may wear it over her heart. Women and men alike may buy love charms from the *newekive*, a curing society potent in magic, black or white. There is a song, too, which men and women may sing "in their heart" to charm the opposite sex. And there is a song which a girl may sing to the corn as she rubs the yellow meal on her face before going out. "Help me," is the substance of it, "I am going to the plaza. Make me look pretty." Rarely do our girls pray, I suppose, when they powder their noses.

Courtship past for the time being, courtship by magic or otherwise, Waiyautitsa is now, let us say, an expectant mother. Her household duties continue to be about the same, but certain precautions, if she inclines to be very circumspect, she does take. She will not test the heat of her oven by sprinkling it in the usual way with bran, for if she does, her child, she has heard, may be born with a skin eruption. Nor will she look at a corpse or help dress a dead animal lest her child be born dead or disfigured. She has heard that even as a little girl if she ate the whitish leaf of the corn husk her child would be an albino. If her husband eat this during the pregnancy the result would be the same. On her husband fall a number of other pregnancy taboos, perhaps as many as fall on her, if not more. If he hunts and maims an animal, the child will be similarly maimed—deformed or perhaps blind. If he joins in a masked dance, the child may have some mask-suggested misshape or some eruption like the paint on the mask. If he sings a great deal, the child will be a cry baby. The habit of thinking in terms of sympathetic magic or of reasoning by analogy which is even more conspicuous at Zuñi than, let us say, at New York, is particularly evident in pregnancy or birth practises or taboos.

Perhaps Waiyautitsa has wished to determine the sex of the child. In that case she may have made a pilgrimage with a rain priest to Towa Yalene, the high mesa three miles to the east of town, to plant a feather-stick which has to be cut and painted in one way for a boy, in another way for a girl. (Throughout the Southwest blue or turquoise is associated with maleness and yellow with femaleness.) Wanting a girl, and girls are wanted in Zuñi quite as much as boys, if not more, Waiyautitsa need not make the trip to the mesa, instead her husband may bring her to wear in her belt scrapings from a stone in a phallic shrine near the mesa. When labor sets in and the pains are slight, indicating, women think, a girl, Waiyautitsa may be told by her mother, "Don't sleep, or you will have a boy." A nap during labor effects a change of sex. When the child is about to be born, Waiyautitsa is careful, too, if she wants a girl, to see that the custom of sending the men out of the house at this time is strictly observed.

After the birth, Waiyautitsa will lie in for several days, four, eight, ten or twelve, according to the custom of her family. Whatever the custom, if she does not observe it, she runs the risk of "drying up" and dying. She lies on a bed of sand heated by hot stones, and upon her abdomen is placed a hot stone. Thus is she "cooked," people say, and creatures whose mothers are not thus treated are called uncooked, raw—they are the animals, the gods, Whites. To be "cooked" seems to be tantamount in Zuñi to being human.

It is the duty of Waiyautitsa's mother-in-law, the child's paternal grandmother, to look after mother and child during the confinement, and at its close to carry the child outdoors at dawn and present him or her to the Sun. Had Waiyautitsa lost children, she might have invited a propitious friend, some woman who had had many children and lost none, to attend the birth and be the first to pick up the child and blow into his mouth. In these circumstances the woman's husband would become the initiator of the child, if a boy, when the child was to be taken into the *kotikyane*. Generally the child's father chooses some man from the house of his own *kuku* or paternal aunt to be the initiator or godfather, so to speak, of the child.

The infant will receive many attentions, too, from his mother and her household. He is placed on a cradle board in which, near the position of his heart, a bit of turquoise is inlaid to preclude the cradle bringing any harm to its tenant. Left alone, a baby runs great risk—some family ghost may come and hold him, causing him to die within four days. And so a quasi fetichistic ear of corn, a double ear thought of as mother and child, is left alongside the baby as a protector. That the baby may teeth promptly, his gums may be rubbed by one who has been bitten by a snake—"snakes want to bite." To make the child's hair grow long and thick, his grandfather or uncle may puff the smoke of native tobacco on his head. That the child may not be afraid in the dark, water-soaked embers are rubbed over his heart the first time he is taken out at night—judging from what I have seen of Zuñi children and adults a quite ineffectual method. That the child may keep well and walk early, hairs from a deer are burned and the child held over the smoke—deer are never sick and rapid is their gait. Their hearing, too, is acute, so discharge from a deer's ear will be put into the baby's ear. That the child may talk well and with tongues, the tongue of a snared mocking-bird may be cut out and held to the baby to lick. The bird will then be released in order that, as it regains its tongue and "talks," the child will talk. A youth who speaks in addition to his native tongue Keresan, English and Spanish has been pointed out to me as one who had licked mocking-bird tongue.

Waiyautitsa will give birth to three or four children, let us say, probably not more, and then, as she approaches middle age, let us suppose she falls sick, and after being doctored unsuccessfully at first by her old father who happens to be a well-known medicine-man of the Great Fire society, and then by a medicine-man from the *newekwa* society whose practice is just the opposite, Waiyautitsa dies. Within a few hours elderly kinswomen of her father's will come in and wash her hair and body, and at dawn sprinkle her face first with water and then with meal. The deceased will be well dressed, and in a blanket donated by her father's people she will be carried to the cemetery lying in front of the old church, a ruin from the days of the Catholic establishment in Zuñi. There to the north of the central wooden cross, *i.e.*, on the north side of the cemetery, Waiyautitsa will be buried. Women are always buried on the north side and men on the south.

Waiyautitsa will be carried out and buried by her father's kinsmen or clansmen. No woman will go to the burial, nor will the widower. The widower, as soon as the corpse is taken outdoors, will be fetched by his women relatives to live at their house. There they straightway wash his hair—a performance inseparable in Zuñi as at other pueblos from every time of crisis or ceremony. The hair of all the other members of Waiyautitsa's household will be washed at the end of four days by women relatives of her father. During this time, since the spirit of Waiyautitsa is thought to linger about the home, the house door will be left open for her at night. The bowl used in washing her hair and the implements used in digging her grave will also be left outdoors. Her smaller and peculiarly personal possessions have been buried with her and bulky things like bedding have been burned or taken to a special place down the river to be buried. The river flows to the lake sixty miles or so west of Zuñi where Waiyautitsa's spirit is also supposed to take its journey. There under the lake it abides except when with other spirits it returns in the clouds to Zuñi to pour down the beneficent rain. People will say to a child, when they see a heavy cloud, "There goes your grandmother," or they will quite seriously say to one another, "Our grandfathers are coming."

Waiyautitsa's children may go on living at home with their grandmother, Waiyautitsa's mother, or it may be one of them is adopted by a maternal aunt or great-aunt or cousin. Zuñi children, cherished possessions as they are, are always being adopted—even in the lifetime of their mother. Adopted, a child—or an adult—will fit thoroughly into the ways of his adoptive household. It is the household as well as the clan which differentiates the Zuñi family group from our individualistic type of family. The household changes quite readily, but whatever its composition, it is an exceedingly integrated and responsible group.

However the children are distributed, it will be the older woman or women in the household who will control them. This household system is one that gives position and considerable authority to the elder women—until the women are too old, people say, to be of any use. (In spite of this irony, I have heard of but one old woman who was neglected by her household.) An older woman who is the female head of the household is greatly respected by her daughters and sons-in-law and grandchildren as well as by the sons or brothers who continually visit the household and often, as temporary celibates, return to live in it.

The older woman is highly esteemed, but she is by no means the head of the household—unless she is widowed. Wherever the household contributes to the ceremonial public life, her husband is paramount. In the non-ceremonial, economic life, too, he has equal, if not greater, authority. And in the general economy he more or less expects his wife to serve him and wait on him. This conjugal subordination is not apparent to any extent among the younger people; the younger husband and wife are too much drawn into the cooperate household life. But as time passes and they in turn become the heads of the household, the man appears to be more given to staying at home, and more and more he takes control.

From this brief survey of the life of a woman at Zuñi in so far as it can be distinguished from the general life, we get the impression that the differentiation of the sexes follows lines of least resistance which start from a fairly fundamental division of labor. From being hunters and trappers men become herders of the domestic animals, drivers or riders. Trade journeys and trips for wood or for the collecting of other natural resources are associated with men, and work on the things acquired is men's work —men, for example, are wood cutters, and bead makers, whether the objects are for secular or sacerdotal use. Analogously all work upon skins or feathers is work for men whether it leads to the manufacture of clothing or to communication with the supernaturals. Again, as farmers, men are associated with that system of supernatural instrumentalism for fertility and weather control which constitutes in large part Zuñi religion. In other words, the bulk of the ceremonial life, a system for the most part of rain rituals, is in the hands of the men. So is government. The secular officers are merely representatives of the priests. Zuñi government is a theocracy in which women have no part. The house and housekeeping are associated with women. Clay is the flesh of a female supernatural and clay processes, brick making or laying or plastering, and pottery making are women's work. There are indications in sacerdotal circles that painting is or was thought of as a feminine activity. Corn, like clay, is the flesh of female supernaturals, and the corn is associated with women. Even men corn growers are in duty bound to bring their product to their wife or mother. Women or women impersonations figure in corn rituals. It is tempting to speculate that formerly, centuries since, women themselves were the corn growers. To-day, at any rate, the preparation of corn as of other food is women's work. Wherever food and its distribution figure in ceremonials, and there is a constant offering of food to the supernaturals, women are apt to figure. Fetiches are attached to houses and in so far as providing for these fetiches is household work it is women's work and leads to the holding of sacerdotal office by women. The household rather than ties of blood is the basis of family life. The children of the household are more closely attached to the women than to the men. One expression of this attachment is seen in reckoning clan membership through the mother.

Household work at Zuñi as elsewhere is continuous. The women are always on the move. The work of the men, on the other hand, is intermittent. Hunting, herding and farming are more or less seasonal activities and are more or less readily fitted into ceremonial pursuits, or rather, in their less urgent periods, take on ceremonial aspects. In the ceremonial life the arts find expression, and the men and not the women are by and large the artists of the tribe.

Attached to the ceremonial life are the games of chance and the races that are played or run at certain seasons. Here again the intermittent habit of work of the men together with their comparative mobility qualify them as gamesters and runners to the exclusion of the women. It is even more unusual to see a Pueblo woman run than to see a white American woman, and like white women, Pueblo Indian women seem quite content to pay no attention to games or merely to look on. They engage in no games.[2]

Household work is confining. Hunting, herding, trading lead to a comparatively mobile habit, a habit of mind or spirit which in the Southwest, at least, is adapted to ceremonial pursuit; for Pueblo Indian ceremonialism thrives on foreign accretions, whether of myth or song or dance or design of mask or costume, or, within certain limits of assimilation, of psychological patterns of purpose or gratification.

To the point of view that the differentiation of the sexes at Zuñi proceeds on the whole from the division of labor the native custom of allowing a boy or man to become, as far as ways of living go, a girl or woman, gives color. Towards adolescence, and sometimes in later life, it is permissible for a boy culturally to change sex. He puts on women's dress, speaks like a woman, and behaves like a woman. This alteration is due to the fact that one takes readily to women's work, one prefers it to men's work. Of one or another of the three men-women now at Zuñi or of the men-women in other pueblos I have always been told that the person in question made the change because he wanted to work like a woman or because his household was short of women and needed a woman worker. This native theory of the institution of the man-woman is a curious commentary, is it not, on that thorough-going belief in the intrinsic difference between the sexes which is so tightly held to in our own culture?

Notes

Originally published in *Scientific Monthly*, No. 9, 1919, pp. 443-57.

1. Analogous reasoning leads to the practise of burning scraps in dress-making that they may not fall into the hands of a witch.
2. Formerly women are said to have played with men a ceremonial or quasi-ceremonial game, a pole and hoop game, and to-day the very little girls, besides playing house, play other games. In one of them the girls trace a spiral on the ground and at the center place a bowl of water to represent a spring. They follow the spiral to get water for their little turkeys which, they sing, are dying of thirst. A "bear" rushes out from the spring and gives chase.

Hopi Mothers and Children

My Sichumovi[1] hostess—in Hopi terms "my sister," since after my head was washed I was regarded as of her clan—the Tansy Mustard (*asnyamo*), had had six girls, and she wanted a boy, so when she was pregnant again, at about the seventh month, she "made a little boy," to hang up in the back room where she kept her other ceremonial things. One of them, the stone fetich animal, the guardian that every Hopi house is possessed[2] of and which is fed daily by the women of the house, I was never shown despite requests,[3] but the doll baby (*tihu*)[4] was promptly exhibited. To my surprise it was not the regular Hopi *tihu, kachina*-like, but, except for the somewhat mask-like face, an out-and-out American doll (*pahan tihu*), about two feet long, dressed in shirt and trousers. A more striking illustration of how the object of foreign material is ever fitted by Pueblo Indians into native pattern would be hard to find. For this American doll had performed the magical function of the *kachina* baby— my sister Anna had born a boy after the pregnancy in question, and, the year following, another boy.

At Hano I was told that a *tihu* is given to a pregnant woman who has lost children[5] and with the *tihu*, although rarely, a miniature cradle may be given. You get a boy *tihu* if you want a boy, a girl *tihu* if a girl.[6] ... At Hano, too, the idea was familiar that a nap during labour will change the sex of the unborn child.[7]

Prayer-stick ritual is also resorted to, as among other Pueblo Indians, when a Hopi woman wants a child and would predetermine the sex. The stick is made at the winter solstice ceremonial (*suyalawun*) by the woman's husband at the time he, as well as every other Hopi man, is in retreat for four days in his home *kiva*,[8] making those cotton strings with soft eagle feathers and pine needles which are called *nakwakwosi* and which all, men, women and children, are going to offer up in this ceremonial in the shrines of the town. Anna appeared unable to describe the prayer-sticks for children; but there was one kind for a boy, she knew, another for a girl, the former being deposited "in a house at Walpi," the latter "in a place at Tewa," a distribution of some interest in the fascinating study of the relations between the towns of the First Mesa.

My bed in the Sichumovi house was under the roof plaque shrine put there eight years ago when the room was rebuilt to entertain the *shalako* masked impersonations. The plaque pieces were unpainted and rudely cut, a contrast to the elaborately painted and carved designs in Zuñi

Facing Page:

Hopi woman at ladder. Photograph by J.R. Willis. Courtesy of the Museum of New Mexico, Negative no. 98191.

houses, and instead of being above the middle of the room, the plaque was at the east side, above the place, I was told, where the *shalako* had sat.   In these *shalako* roof shrines at Zuñi[9] are placed prayer-sticks to represent offspring, a prayer for offspring to increase the household.[10] These sticks in the plaque of my room had been taken and buried under the floor, since boarded over. Were the sticks of the Zuñi type or of the quite different Hopi type? It is a detail, like other details of this borrowed Zuñi ceremonial, of no little interest to the student of diffusion in ceremonialism.

Zuñi pregnancy taboos occur on the First Mesa with interesting variations. The prospective father may not hurt horses or cows or shoot rabbits, lest blood run from the baby's nose at birth or the baby cry incessantly. As cure the father should take wool or hair from the injured animal, set fire to it and hold the baby under a blanket over the smoke. If the baby is disfigured, is born with a twisted mouth, for example, like some *kachina* mask, a bit should be scraped from the mask and set fire to, the baby held, as in the preceding case, over the smoke.[11] The belief that albinism was caused by eating the white leaf of corn was familiar at Hano, unfamiliar at Sichumovi. There are no albinos on the First Mesa; but, as I noticed, there are four, perhaps more, on the Second Mesa. Incidentally, I may note that Anna of Sichumovi had never seen these albinos, as she and her daughters had never been to the Second Mesa towns, towns only from six to eight miles distant. Truly Pueblo Indian women are home stayers!

As to twins, non-naturalistic beliefs seem scanty. None of the twin beliefs heard elsewhere in other pueblos was familiar. At Hano, "a pregnant woman going with another man has twins," some say, a saying learned, one suspects, from the white.

To hasten labour a weasel (*piwani*) is passed four times over the "stomach" and down—the weasel goes in and out quickly. In the Hano house I visited, a weasel skin hung on the wall; it was the one my acquaintance used in labour.[12] Obviously this device for an easy delivery is a personal one, not a specific of the Badger clansman in Hano who "knows how to take out babies," and who is summoned by all the women of both Hano and Sichumovi at childbirth.[13] "If you are in pain because the baby lies wrong, he puts it straight," and he stays until after the birth. He also sets bones, having learned how from another old man. He is a Hopi man although he lives at Hano, and he is own brother to the only man who is called a doctor (Hopi, *duiyka*, Tewa, *masoix* or *wolokanix*) on the mesa. Cures are associated with their ceremonies by the Hopi, but, on the whole, Hopi curing ritual appears less conspicuous than the curing ritual of the other Pueblo Indian tribes.

Hopi child with kachina, August 1938. Photograph by Harold Kellogg. Courtesy of the Museum of New Mexico, Negative no. 77536.

Hopi piki maker, ca. 1911. Photograph by H.F. Robinson. Courtesy of the Museum of New Mexico, Negative no. 21607.

The placenta is thrown away down the edge of the north-eastern cliff where dead babies are thrown. Adults are buried in set places at the foot of the mesa, each town having its own burial place. "The *muki* (a derisive term supposed to mean the dead, applied to the Hopi by the other tribes) used to throw all the dead into holes in the rocks," a Santo Domingan once observed to me. Possibly from an imputation of this kind was derived the term *muki*.

When the cord falls, fine ashes are put on the navel, and the cord is tied, for a girl, to a *silkuh*, the stick to stir corn-meal in cooking, that the girl may cook well; for a boy, to an arrow, that he may shoot rabbits, and, thus set, the cord is put on the roof of the house.[14] At Laguna desire to predetermine qualifications in the child is likewise expressed, but here the cord is buried under the house floor near the grinding-stones, in case of a girl; in the middle of a field, in case of a boy—a variation in dispoal, due, perhaps, to the encroachment of agriculture, among men's occupations, upon the hunt.

For the first four days an ear of white corn, completely kernelled, is left alongside the baby.[15] It is "his mother,"—by this term is ever described the ceremonial ear of corn called *yapota* at Zuñi, *kotona* by the Keres, *pohtsele* by the Tewa, and *chotsm wa* by the Hopi.

The confinement lasts twenty days, as does the wedding ceremonial, we may note incidentally, where the bride is thought of as re-born. As soon as the baby is born, the paternal grandmother is summoned. She washes the baby and covers it with ashes as a depilatory.[16] Hereafter she washes the baby every morning.... For about one day after the birth the mother will not try to suckle the child. If the birth is in the morning, she will start to nurse at midnight; if at night, the following afternoon.... The mother is well covered up after the birth, that there may be plenty of milk.... Only corn-meal mush is fed to her. It is cooked for her morning and evening by the paternal grandmother. During the whole confinement the mother may take neither salt nor meat—a restriction which in all the pueblos constitutes ceremonial fasting—and she may drink only water boiled with juniper (*onmapi*), a brew which is also supplied by the paternal grandmother.[17]

After four days the paternal grandmother washes the clothes of mother and baby and early in the morning of the fifth day she washes the mother's head, and gives her a sweat bath. She heats a stone in the stove, and puts the stone covered over with juniper into a bowl; pouring on water, she places the mother over the bowl, so that the steam goes up "into her" and she sweats. Again, on the ninth day the paternal grandmother washes clothes and on the tenth the head of the mother, giving her a sweat bath. On the tenth day the mother may walk about and "grind corn for the baby" (?). On the fourteenth day the paternal grandmother washes the clothes and on the fifteenth day the head of the mother, giving the sweat bath. On the nineteenth day the paternal grandmother washes the clothes, and on this day the wife of the mother's brother or maternal uncle comes to the house to make wafer-bread (*piki*) and *pigami* (meal that is cooked overnight).[18] This evening all the women of the neighbourhood, related and unrelated,[19] carry bowls of meal to the mother's house.

On the twentieth morning, before sunrise, the paternal grandmother and the paternal aunts of the baby, *i.e.*, theoretically all the women in his father's clan, come to the house to carry out the ceremony of *asnaya, i.e.,* to wash the head of the baby and give him a name. First the mother's head and body are washed by the paternal grandmother. The head washing of the baby is first done ritually by each woman dipping the yucca root suds on to the head with an ear of corn, holding the ear by the piece of stalk which has been left attached. The dipping is done four times, and, I surmise, a brief prayer is said, perhaps only by the first to dip, perhaps by all, and a clan song is sung by a clansman to whom is known the *asnaya* song that every clan is possessed of. It was in this ritualistic fashion that my own head was washed, as is the head of any foreigner, white or Indian, who is considered eligible for a friendly relationship.

After the head washing, the paternal grandmother rubs the baby all over with corn meal. ("My father's" sister rubbed the meal on my face and chest.) Then the grandmother gives the baby to the mother to hold and each woman in the father's clan[20] proceeds to give the child a present, also a name. Again, from my own experience and the Oraibi account I surmise that together with the name the officiator gives a blessing or good wish,[21] and that, as she speaks, she moves the corn ear in a circle four times in front of the child.

After the naming, for the first time the baby is laid on a new cradle[22]—before that he lay on some old cradle—they tie him in and put four ears of corn in the cradle. In this cradle the paternal grandmother carries the baby out, timing the exit with sunrise, the mother accompanying them. The women sprinkle meal, and the grandmother says, "You have come out to see the sun," calling the baby by name. By which of his perhaps thirty or more names appears uncertain, perhaps by the name the grandmother herself bestowed. Which name is going "to stick" seems always to be indefinite, a matter of fancy.

The Company now eats the meal of *pigami* and meat, and each visitor is given a bowl of meal to take home. It is on this occasion that the salt and meat restriction on the baby's mother is lifted.

The foregoing account is from a Hopi woman in Sichumovi. I got an account from a Tewa woman at Hano, which varies only in adding several particulars which I think were merely omitted in the Hopi account.... The mother (*yiya*) is steamed "to make the sickness all come out." ... At first

Postcard image of famous Hopi potter Nampeyo at Hano ca. 1910. Courtesy of the Museum of New Mexico, Negative no. 40327.

the juniper brew is hot; every four[23] days it is made less hot and with it, as it grows cooler, you grow stronger.... The mother never goes barefoot lest she gets cold.[24] On the nineteenth day the baby's father (*dada*) will kill a sheep for the mother to eat.... Were the brother's or uncle's wife (*saii'*) not to come to make *pigami* (Tewa, *mowakoke'*) the mother's own household would make it.... On the twentieth day the mother's face, as well as the baby's, is rubbed with corn meal.... Each of the paternal clanswomen (*kiyiyuin*) gives an ear of corn as well as another present of quilt, clothing, etc. Three of these ears of corn are placed in the cradle.... A line of corn meal (*kunlu kili*, corn coarse)[25] is sprinkled from the cradle to the door and the encradled baby is carried out over this meal line, the paternal grandmother waving the cradle gently as they go out to pray to the Sun and give him thanks.... The paternal grandmother receives a specially large quota of meal—a large basket or American boiler full.... They call out to the neighbours to come and eat at the house of the baby, referring to him by name, "that is how they learn his name." On the twenty-fourth day the paternal grandmother again washes the clothes, and on the twenty-fifth day the mother's head is washed with cold water for the first time and she is given cold water to drink. "...If you feel well during the twenty days you may walk around a little and cook," concluded my informant, "but you must not go outdoors.[26] You get tired staying in the house in summer; the winter is a nice time to have a baby; then you stay indoors anyhow."

A baby is about two months old before it is carried on the back. Before it is put in this position for the first time someone will take a man's moccasin, if the baby is a boy, a woman's moccasin, if a girl, and with it slap the mother on her back four times.[27]

As elsewhere, reluctance is felt about leaving the baby alone, lest one of the dead (*isatsihnumo*) come and hold the baby and the baby die.[28] A brush of twigs, the common house brush, will be left alongside the baby as protector.

No device was known to make a child learn to walk except an American walking-machine, which was a curiously conspicuous object hanging from the rafters of my room—rafters which also harboured not only the *shalako* shrine I mentioned, but many of the red prayer-sticks made each winter by the *kalehktaka* or warrior priest to strengthen the houses of the mesa. To get the child to talk well a bird, called *yaupa*,[29] would be held four times to the child's mouth, and then released. The Zuñi elaboration of cutting out the bird's tongue[30] was unfamiliar and aroused condemnation.

If a baby has earache, a member of the *lenawimi*, the Flute ceremony, and one who has been lightning shocked,[31] is summoned to blow four times into the baby's ear. It is the rite of breath expulsion the Keres call *kaiashats*, which at Laguna is employed by a snake-bitten man against sore navel. Sore navel at Zuñi is also treated by the snake-bitten.[32]

Older children are told that their ears will ache if they sing the *kachina* songs.... As elsewhere, the *kachina* give bows and arrows to the boys and dolls to the girls. Other presents,[33] too, come from or rather through[34] the *kachina.* "We give the *kachina* things to give the children if they are good. We ask the children what they want, and we go to the store and buy it and give it to the *kachinas* to give to the children. We say to the children, 'Now you see when you are good, you get what you want.'"...At the *niman kachina* ceremony in July, cattails are given by the *kachina* to the children from which a chewing gum is made. (The practice is Zuñi, too.)

Kachina gifts to the children are discontinued after the children have been whipped, *i.e.*, exorcised at the *powamu* ceremony. Children of six or seven are "whipped," or to-day even younger children, since, as my informant naively put it, "it is hard to get children the presents they want." ...The child holds a *nakwakwosi* in the hand while being whipped. For the three days following he or she may eat no food with salt in it. At the time of whipping they learn that the *kachina* are men, or rather impersonated by men, for their supernatural character is still emphasized. "We tell them that the *kachinas* come from the waters.[35] If they tell the younger children the *kachinas* are men, more *kachinas* will come to whip them, and this time they will be the real *kachinas* and, we say, 'They will cut off your head and throw it on top of the house.'"[36]

Reality is given to this threat by the *shuyuku* or giant *kachina*, "a crowd of them."[37] During *powamu* they pay their domiciliary visits just as at the same season, about February, their Zuñi homologue, the *atoshle* goes about.[38] Like *atoshle*, *shuyuku* carries a knife, a bow and arrow, and on his back a basket. He tells the children to mind their parents, "otherwise I will carry you home in my basket and my children will eat you up. At home now there is a fire ready to cook you."...Among his intimidating comments *shuyuku* will say to the children, "Children, I know what you are like, sometimes you come to the fireplace and you hit my eye with a stick." *Shuyuku* is said to live in the fire —a device to keep the little ones away from it,[39] just as at Zuñi, to protect the peaches against juvenile poachers, the *suuke* of the caves are said to haunt the peach orchards at the foot of the mesas.

The frightened children will give *shuyuku* presents to make him go away. First they will give him a mouse "to try him," at last mutton "to make a friend of him." I am reminded of a Zuñi friend who found a pest of grasshoppers this year in his field. Grasshoppers are witch-sent, so every morning my friend would bury a little corn meal in the field "to pay the grasshoppers to go away."

At *powamu* a boy gets the name that theoretically, at least, will supersede his baby name and be his lifelong name. The name is given to him by the man, any friend or relative of the family, chosen to be his "father" or initiator. I heard of a baby boy who was sick, and who was therefore "given" to the husband of his mother's sister to be sponsored by him in coming years at the *powamu* ceremony, and still later, when the boy is fourteen or fifteen, in the ceremony to which the man himself belongs, one of the four ceremonies into one of which every youth must be initiated before he can take part in the great tribal ceremony of the winter solstice. Girls are not put into these ceremonies; at *powamu* it is their father's sister who sees them through.[40]

Notes

Originally published in *Man*, No. 58, July 1921, pp. 98-104. The original footnote symbols have been converted to numerals and numbered consecutively as endnotes..

1. One of the three towns on the First or East Mesa of the Hopi of Arizona. The two other towns are Walpi and Hano.
2. At Zuni and among the Keres such fetich animals are in the possession of the curing societies. (Cp. Parsons, E. C., "Notes on Ceremonialism at Laguna," *Anthropological Papers, American Museum of Natural History*, vol. XIX, pt. IV, fig. 20.)
3. Barbara Freire-Marecco had had a like experience, I was told, while she lived at Hano, the adjacent town peopled by Tewa immigrants from New Mexico. The house next to Miss Freires-Marecco's was a Bear clan house, and contained the fetich mask of the Tewa Bear clan. "I would *never* let that English woman, or any white people, see it," declared with the utmost conviction its male guardian, a chief in the Tewa Bear clan.
4. *Tihpusi,* baby. At Zuni and Laguna there is an identical term for doll and baby.
5. At Oraibi on the Third or West Mesa, in the *powamu* ceremony old women impersonations carry doll babies towards which sterile women "and also others" sprinkle meal, towards a boy doll if a boy baby is desired, towards a girl doll if a girl baby. (Voth, H. R., "The Oraibi Powamu Ceremony," 121, *Field Columbian Mus. Pub.*, 61, Anthropological Series III, 2, 1901.) Pl. LXXIII. *d.'* represents a girl doll, except in dress, not unlike the boy doll, sister Anna said she had made for herself.

    Cp. Dumarest, Noël, "Notes on Cochiti, New Mexico," p. 141 and Fig. 3 (*Memoirs American Anthropological Association*, vol. VI, No. 3, 1919).
6. Zuni practice (Parsons, E. C., "Mothers and Children at Zuni, New Mexico," MAN, 1919, **86**).
7. Zuni belief (MAN, 1919, **86**).
8. The ceremonial club house of the men. Men marry away from home and frequent the *kiva* near their wife's house; they also, as members of certain ceremonies, make use of *kivas* loaned for the ceremony; but at the winter solstice they are required to repair to the *kiva* habitually used by their own clan in their own town.
9. Parsons, E. C., "Notes on Zuni," *Memoirs American Anthropological Association*, Vol. IV, No. 3, p. 193, 1917.
10. During the summer ceremonies of the Snake and Antelope Societies on the Second Mesa prayer-sticks are deposited that many children may "be born in the village." (Dorsey, G. A., and Voth, H. R., "The Mishongnovi Ceremonies of the Snake and Antelope Fraternities," 234, *Field Columbian Museum Pub.* 66, Anthropological Series, vol. III, No. 3, 1902.)
11. Cp. MAN, 1919, **86**.
12. Cp. Owens, I. G., "Natal Ceremonies of the Hopi Indians," *Journal American Ethnology and Archaeology*, II (1892), 165.

    According to Voth, the meat of the *piwani,* the fat or a bit of skin, is given to the women in labour as medicine "that the child may come out quickly." The animal lacking, a herb (*Linum rigidum Pursh*) may be used and called *piwanna, piwani* medicine. ("The Oraibi Soyal Ceremony," 34 fol., *Field Columbian Museum Pub.* 55, Anthrop. Ser., vol. III, No. I, 1901; "Oraibi Natal Customs and Ceremonies," *Field Columbian Mus. Pub.* 97, Anthrop. Ser., vol. VI, No. 2, p. 51.) Of analogous substituting, plant for animal, I have heard at Zuñi.

    Weasel skins are attached to insignia of the Snake and Antelope Societies, and weasel medicine is part of the antidote to snake-bite. (Voth, H. R., "The Oraibi Summer Snake Ceremony," p. 354, *Field Columbian Mus. Pub.* 83, Anthrop. Ser. III, No. 4, 1903.)

13. The badger is associated with childbirth at Laguna, and by the Hopi the badger is supposed to have control of all medicinal roots. (Voth, H. R., "Hopi Proper Names," *Field Columbian Mus. Pub.* 100, Anthrop. Ser., vol. VI, No. 3, p. 80.)

14. "Thrust behind some joist of the house," writes Voth. And the cord has been severed on this same arrow or stirring stick (*Oraibi Natal Customs and Ceremonies*, p. 48).

15. Laguna practice (MAN, 1919, **86**). At Oraibi two ears of corn brought by the paternal grandmother are left alongside for twenty days (*Oraibi Natal Customs and Ceremonies*, p. 49).

16. Zuñi practice (MAN, 1919, **86**).

17. *Ibid.*

18. In an underground oven (J.A.E.A., II, 167). According to Owens, a stew of mutton and shelled corn is also prepared.

19. In the agricultural working parties unrelated neighbours may also co-operate.

20. In his general account Voth refers in this connection to the women of the mother's clan; but in his account of a particular ceremony the women are of the father's clan (*Oraibi Natal Customs and Ceremonies*, pp. 54, 58-9).

21. *Yan ommachiukyüng wüwyv'mihakamiix' ox katchi nawuh'kyauwintani.*
    thus named get to be old life prosperous

    The Oraibi formula is similar and Voth translates: "To old age your life being preserved may you become an old man, but you shall be named" (*Oraibi Natal Customs and Ceremonies*, p. 54). For the same formula in initiation into the Snake and Antelope Societies see *The Mishongnovi Ceremonies of the Snake and Antelope Fraternities*, 246. Cp. the Zuñi baptismal prayer (MAN, 1919, **86**).

22. Zuñi practice (MAN, 1919, **86**). The cradle is wicker, made of *siwiwibi* or *silobi* [*Rhu. trilobata* according to Owens, who called it by its berry, *siwipsi* (*sibibsi*)]. "They would be afraid to use lightning-riven wood" as is used at Laguna.

23. Every five days (Hopi).

24. Oraibi practice. Cp. *Oraibi Natal Customs and Ceremonies*, p. 53, also pp. 50-52. The desire to keep the mother warm is expressed even more emphatically at Zuñi, where the woman is said to be "cooked."

25. Cp. J.A.E.A., II., 168, N.L. Several interesting little rites are described by Owens, which my informants ignored—marking the walls of the house, the ceiling, and the floor, with four parallel lines (done at Oraibi also); placing a *nakwakwosi* under a bowl the head is washed in; waving this bowl four times in a horizontal circle and throwing it, together with the sweepings from the floor, a piece of sheepskin from the mother's bed, the *nakwakwosi*, and a live coal, off the mesa top—all these rites among the Hopi; among the Tewa, the giving of medicine-water and the throwing of a coal off the mesa by the mother, who thereupon turns round four times in anti-sunwise circuit.

    For sunrise rites at Oraibi see *Oraibi Natal Customs and Ceremonies*, pp. 56-6, 60-1. The ritualistic waving from the East recalls Laguna practice (Parsons, E. C., "Mothers and Children at Laguna, New Mexico," MAN, 1919, **18**).

26. According to Owens, the woman may go out on the fifth day; according to Voth, "a primapara is not allowed to leave the house before sundown during the entire puerperal period, while a multipara may do so occasionally after the fifth day" (*Oraibi Natal Customs and Ceremonies*, p. 53). Both Owens and Voth refer to hanging a curtain over the door to keep out the sunlight, for four days according to Owens, for twenty days according to Voth. Nowadays windows are shaded.

27. At Zuñi it is the child that is whipped (MAN, 1919, **86**).

28. Zuñi belief (MAN, 1919, **86**).

29. Unfortunately there is confusion over the identity of this bird. Voth states that the feather is used in war ritual and he thinks that it may be the vermilion flycatcher (*The Oraibi Powamu Ceremony*, p. 77). Fewkes gives a bird *kachina* with vermilion feathers, called *yaupa* or mocking-bird, in "Hopi Katcinas," pl. XVII, *Twenty-first Annual Report of the Bureau of Ethnology*, 1904. Now the mocking-bird is grey, white and black, without

vermilion. My guess is that holding the bird to the child's mouth may have been originally to endow the child as a warrior, and that *yaupa* is associated with the war chief because of its black streak across the eyes.

30. MAN, 1919, **86**.

31. The Flute ceremony belong to the millet clan, who are *ipso facto* members of the ceremony; but any one shocked by lightning, or any owner of a field struck by lightning, or the household of a stricken house, is initiated into the ceremony.

32. Voth describes a curing rite for infants performed by members of the Snake Fraternity without stating the nature of the ailment (*The Mishongnovi Ceremonies of the Snake and Antelope Fraternities*, p. 253).

33. To adults, too, the masked impersonators at Zuñi and among the Keres are primarily present-givers. They give rain and crops. What they throw out to the onlookers at the dances and give in domiciliary visits to the children are expressions of this concept.

34. Cp. MAN, 1919, **18.**

35. From *kisiwuhpa*, a spring on *gumatuxtekwi*, Black Mountain, the adults themselves believe.

36. Throw it to *kothluwela*, the home of the Zuñi *koko* or *kachina*, Zuñi boys are told.

37. Generally four, at Oraibi, *shooyoktu,* elder brother, uncle (2), and *shooyoktu,* woman (*The Oraibi Powamu Ceremony*, 118).

38. *See* Parsons, E. C., "The Zuñi A'doshle and Suuke," *American Anthropologist*, XVIII (1915), 338-347.

39. It is said that a child will be a "fire meddler" if the fire kept burning during the confinement period is allowed to go out or if anything is baked in this fire (*Oraibi Natal Customs and Ceremonies*, p. 52). . . .At Cochiti a fire is kept up during the confinement (*Dumarest,* p. 143).

40. That is among the Tewa, I have learned since this article was written; among the Hopi, girls as well as boys are "given" to a ceremonial father.

    Another recent piece of information is that the conception of twins results from intercourse in daylight, one child being imputed to the sun. "We know this from an old story." The twin children of the sun do in fact figure in Pueblo Indian folklore.

    Likewise I have learned that only old persons would eat the meat of an unborn calf. Since the foetus is blind; were a woman of child-bearing age to eat the meat, her offspring might be born blind.

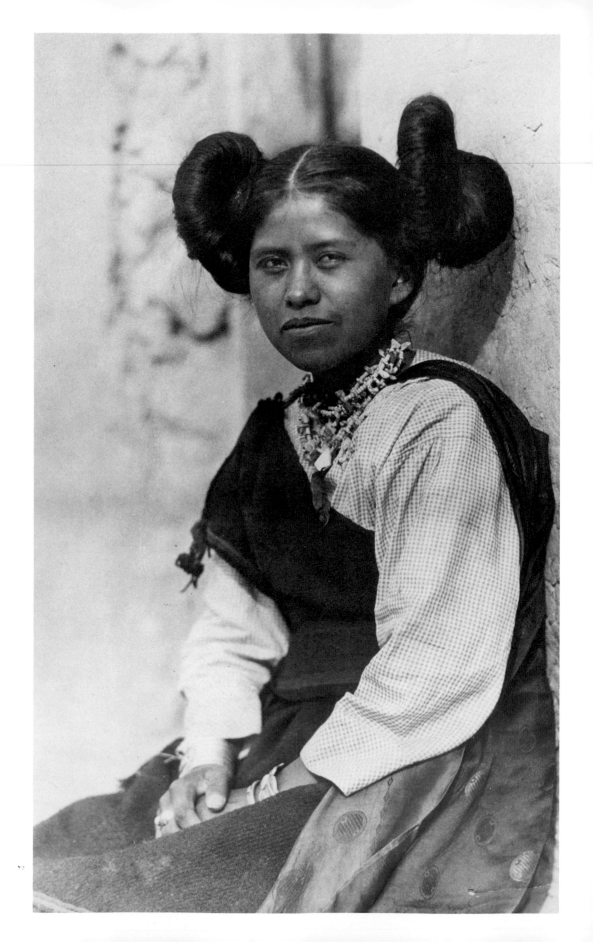

Getting Married on First Mesa, Arizona

There are three towns or rather two towns and a suburb on First or East Mesa, Walpi, the Hopi town, with its suburb Sichumovi, and Hano or Tewa, a Tanoan settlement from the East, made, it is said, two hundred or more years ago.

It was from Yellow-pine, a young Tewa woman married for about three years that I heard most about Tewa wedding practices. Yellow-pine spoke English comparatively well, well enough to tell a story in English in about the same way as she would tell it in Tewa. This is her narrative:

"The boy goes to the girl's house at night to see her. If the girl's mother does not want him, she tells the girl. If she wants him, she says, 'You can talk[1] to him, she says. (But if the girl wants the boy, even if her people do not want him, she can talk to him.) The boy tells his people; if they say yes, then the boy comes again and tells the girl. Then the girl makes *piki* [wafer bread, in Tewa, *mowa*], the narrow kind of *piki*, like sticks (*makana*). She makes *piki* all day. She piles it high, beginning early in the morning. At night the girl and her mother take the *piki* to the boy's house. The boy's people are happy and say, 'Thank you,' and give them meat. They bring it home. From that they all know that he is going to marry her. Now, any night, they take *piki* again to the boy's house, and the boy's people give meat. From then on they begin to get married....

They grind corn every day until they fill ten or twelve boilers [store-bought tin boilers]. It takes a month to complete that work. They also prepare white corn to put in water for the boys to drink. Then they are ready. They go to the boy's house to tell the boy's people they will come in four days. The boy's people get things ready to eat. The girl tells her uncles [maternal uncles or kinsmen] and fathers [paternal kinsmen] to come to her house on the night they plan for....

On this night they dress the girl in her *manta* [i.e. ceremonial blanket] and wheel her hair. Then they go to the boy's house where all the boy's people are gathered together, and where they have set out meat and bread and coffee. 'We have brought this girl to you to grind as much

Facing Page:

Hopi girl with "nasumtah," the butterfly whorl hair arrangement of unmarried women. Photograph by J.R. Willis. Courtesy of the Museum of New Mexico, Negative no. 98184.

as she can,' say the girl's uncles. 'Is that so? All right. We are glad to have her,' they say. . . .

Next day, early in the morning, the girl starts to grind. She has to grind all day,[2] stopping only to eat. For three days the girl grinds. Early in the morning of the fourth day they wash the girl's head. The girl grinds once more and finishes. They [in the girl's house] make many bowls of blue corn meal, and they make *mowasi* (corn boiled and wrapped in corn husk). The girl's clanswomen come in to help. That night the girl's people take to the girl's house five or six boilers [empty] from which they are to give out meal to the boy's people, his aunts [father's sisters], uncles, and mothers [mother's sisters or kinswomen], meal and *piki* and on top *mowasi*. Whatever is left over is given to the boy's mother.

That day the boy's clansmen have brought out cotton to weave into a blanket for the girl. They take the cotton to the girl's house. Her mother thanks them, and puts meal for them in the bowl that held the cotton. The men take the cotton to the kiva to work on it. While they work, the girl has to stay on in the boy's house and do the cooking of the house and the sweeping, while they work for her in the kiva. . . .

When the men in the kiva start to make the white blanket, they take *piki* to them and white corn water to drink. And every day they take bread and meat. At the girl's house they are making heaps of meal and the girl's clanswomen are making *piki*, all night the women are making *piki*, and all night there is a meal set out for them. The next night they make *pigami* (a stew of samp and mutton).

A day or two later they take water to the girl's house and to the boy's house to get ready to make *piki* early in the morning. In both houses they make *piki* to take to the houses of the men who are working in the kiva for the girl. In that way they pay the men for making things for the girl.

Then the boy's mother tells the girl's mother in how many nights they are going to take the girl home again. They get ready, they cook for that night. . . . They put on the girl her blanket and moccasins. That night they cut the girl's hair on the sides.[3] The boy's mother and sisters take the girl to the girl's house. There, to thank them, are assembled the girl's uncles.

Early the next morning, they wash the boy's head [he has followed his wife], all the girl's mothers and father's sisters wash his head.

Four days later they make *piki* all day in the girl's house and towards evening they take it all to the boy's house. . . .

Afterwards, at any time, perhaps two or three years afterwards, the girl has ground in her house ten boilerfuls of corn, including one boilerful of white corn and one of sweet corn. After this grinding, the boy's people go to the girl's house and whitewash the walls and clean house. The next day the boy's mothers and father's sisters bring water to the girl's house. The next day, early in the morning, in the girl's house they start to make *piki*. They make *piki* and they grind meal all day. They fill up the baskets to take them to the boy's mothers. With a pan of beans the girl's mother goes first, the girl in her white blanket follows and the other women. The boy's people are waiting, they get happy. They go to the girl's house and eat. That is all, except that afterwards, at any time when the men who made her things are going to dance, the girl dresses in her white blanket and takes the dancers *pigami*.[4]—It is hard work for us to get married.

A long time ago, it was not so hard. But now we get married just like Hopi, and it is much longer and harder."

It is quite likely, as Yellow-pine suggested, that Tewa marriage ceremonial was formerly more simple, as it is among other Pueblo Indian peoples. In Tewa folk-tales the ceremonial or etiquette of getting married is much the same as in Zuni tale and practice[5] and probably in ancient Keresan practice.[6] The youth comes to the girl's house. She sets food out for him, he tells the parents what he has come for, they say that it is not for them to say, but for their daughter. (As Yellow-pine remarked, the choice is really with the girl.[7]) The youth leaves, to return another night with his bundle, his gifts of blankets, belt, and moccasins to the girl. If she accepts them, she carries in her turn a gift of corn meal to the young man's house, where she stays four days to grind. There on the fourth morning her head is washed. Then the couple return to live at the house of the girl's mother. A gift of apparel from the man, a gift of meal from the girl, her visit, a betrothal visit, so to speak, to the man's maternal house, the rite of head washing, and the return to the girl's maternal house—this seems to be the generic Pueblo form of wedding to which the Hopi and then the Tewa, in imitation, gave elaboration. Curiously enough, Spanish influence in the Eastern pueblos, Keresan and Tanoan,[8] has tended to a somewhat analogous elaboration, a case of similarity, we can but think, due to convergence.

The extent of the Hopi elaboration appears even more fully in another account of Hopi wedding practices given me by a Tewa man, a Bear clansman married into a Hopi (Sichumovi) house and the father of a girl whose wedding was not yet completed, although she was the mother of a three months' old infant. The final gift of meal was not yet made. My Tewa friend had the wedding of his daughter Butterfly in mind, as he talked, I think, although he put his narrative into an impersonal form. Some of his narrative is supplemented by information from his wife, Butterfly's mother.

Whenever a girl finds a boy, the boy comes to see the girl's parents. After he comes, the parents ask what he wants. "I come to see about your daughter," he says. "I don't know about it," says the father of the girl, also the mother of the girl. "We will tell her uncles (*taamato*, her mother's brothers, etc.), and see what they have to say" ... The mother of the girl tells her uncles to come to her house. They come at the time she says. (There were six uncles who came in to talk about Butterfly). The mother of the girl says, 'I called you because there is a boy wants our child. I told him I had nothing to say until I called you.' An uncle may say, 'I don't think we want that boy to marry our niece (*tatiwaiya*, sister's child).' Or an uncle may say, 'Well, it is all right.' [In this case] the next time the boy comes, the mother of the girl says, 'I told my uncles. It is all right, they say. Tell your mother and father, and they will tell your uncles, and what your uncles say you tell us.' Then the mother of the boy will call in her uncles and tell them that the boy has been to the girl's house. 'Her mother and father said for me to call you and see what you think about it'... If it is all right, the girl's people take some food (*piki*) to the boy's house to let them know that the girl is going to marry the boy. This *piki* the boy's mother distributes to all members of her clan.... After this the parents of the boy have to look for buckskin, and for cotton to weave into the wedding blankets (*kwatskyapa*)... The girl's people begin to grind corn to fill ten bowls. (To help Butterfly, there were, besides her mother and mother's mother and mother's sister, one other close relative and five clanswomen). Then they say when they will take the girl to the boy's house; they tell the mother of the girl to tell the mother of the boy. The mother of the girl goes and tells the mother of the boy, and she tells all her uncles to come to her house and all her clanswomen (*nahimato*) and all the aunts (*kyamato*, father's sisters) of the girl and all the girl's father's brothers (*namato*) i.e. clansmen. (When our girl married only my own two brothers came, but we asked all the Bear men. We can't tell who will come.)[9] The girl's aunts take some corn meal to the girl's house, in the evening, and the aunt[10] of the girl dresses the girl and puts her hair up in wheels. They all talk to the girl, each of them saying she must work at the boy's house and not be lazy.... They go to the boy's house, the girl's aunt goes first, carrying corn meal on her back, then the girl, then the girl's mother and then the girl's father, then the uncles, then the girl's brothers. They all go single file—[the usual Hopi formation for any formal group in progress]. At the boy's house they have prepared supper for all who are to come. They eat supper, they leave the girl there, they go back home. This night the mother of the boy takes care of the girl. Early in

the morning the girl gets up to grind corn. Across the place where the girl is grinding they hang a blanket or, nowadays, a wagon cover, so nobody may talk to her or the sun shine on her. They give her breakfast.... The boy's father's mother tells all her clanswomen to go to the boy's house, carrying water. The boy's mother goes around and invites her clanswomen to come to help her against the boy's father's clanswomen. Then they start to fight. (*Moungkipoh mowa*, female connection by marriage; *kipoh,* go to fight). [See below for explanation]. Then they go back home.... The girl grinds all day. The mother of the boy tells the girl when to stop grinding. They eat supper, they go to bed, and the mother of the boy takes care of the girl.... The first day the girl grinds white corn, the second and third days, blue corn, the fourth day, pop corn to be drunk in water. On the third day, in the evening, the mother of the girl begins to put up her meal to take to the boy's house. The father or brother of the girl are to take it to the boy's house. All night any of the townswomen may go to the girl's house to help make *piki*[11] as well as the girl's clanswomen, even clanswomen from other towns.... Early in the morning they wash the girl's head; first the mother of the boy takes down one wheel of the girl's hair

Hopi girl having her hair put into butterfly whorls, ca. 1920. Photograph by Elsie Clews Parsons. Courtesy of the American Philosophical Society.

and washes, then the father of the boy takes down the other wheel and washes, then the boy's sisters wash and then his clanswomen.[12] [They wash, as usual, with jucca root suds, dipping the suds on the head with an ear of white corn that is completely kernelled, one of the ears people refer to as "mother" and which is used on many ceremonial occasions. The dipping is quite formal, the head touched lightly four times, when a few words of prayer may be said. A thorough washing follows. After the washing, corn meal is rubbed on face, arms, and body, and meal is given to the person washed to take out and sprinkle, perhaps in a shrine, or on the eastern edge of the mesa, with a prayer for long life and prosperity.] They dress the girl's hair in a roll along each side of the head.[13]

After the head washing they eat the *piki* brought from the girl's house and the *pigami* made in the boy's house and for which his father has killed a cow. Other *piki* is given later in the day to the boy's clanswomen who come in to wash the girl's head, *piki* and on top of it *chakobiki*, sweet corn meal, which is to be drunk in water.

Then the boy's uncles (*taamato*) and the boy's father's brothers (*namato*) [i.e. clansmen] bring in cotton to spin and weave for the girl. The girl's mother who is in the boy's house refills the baskets holding the cotton with corn meal, in return for the cotton. The cotton is divided into four piles, the father of the boy is to make one *oba* (white blanket with red and black border), the boy's uncle, an *oba* and an *ato*, (larger white blanket, embroidered), and the boy's father's brother a belt (*wokukwewa*). [They may also make a dress of black wool]. They take the cotton to the kiva, to spin[14] and weave. They don't know how long it will take—several days, sometimes a month, sometimes less. (For Butterfly they were spinning three days, and weaving three days). During this time the girl is grinding or making *piki* in the boy's house, where her clanswomen come to help her. This is for the men at work in the kiva to eat. They take the *piki* to them every afternoon, and sweet corn meal in water. Besides, at this time, the boy's clanspeople come to the boy's house to eat. Whatever corn meal or *piki* is left over is given to the guests to carry away with them, [as is usual in Pueblo Indian circles when a meal is thought of as pay in kind.]

Through with weaving, they make the moccasins, perhaps the boy's father makes them, perhaps his uncle. The night of the day they finish making the moccasins, they take the girl back to her house, first dressing her up in her new things, and the boy follows her. For all of them, the mother of the girl has a meal ready. Earlier in the day the boy's mother has carried the girl's mother a basket of corn. Before the boy leaves his house, his people talk to him, telling him not to be lazy and to be good to everybody in his wife's house—"that is why he is getting married."

Hopi woman Moqko in bridal garments, holding a reed container for clothing woven by men of the bridegroom's family. Oraibi, 1901. Photograph by Carl N. Werntz. Courtesy of the Museum of New Mexico, Negative no. 37543.

Lakon Harvest Dance at Walpi, Fall, 1920. Photograph by Elsie Clews Parsons. Courtesy of the American Philosophical Society.

Early the next morning [after the night return to the girl's house] the clanswomen of the girl come in to wash the boy's head, just as the girl's head has been washed. Three days later the boy has to get wood. On the fourth day the girl's clanswomen come in to make *piki* all day. That evening they take the *piki* to the boy's house. The following evening those *piki* makers return to the girl's house to which the boy's mother brings some *piki* and meat for them to eat. That is the end of it....

If the girl is married in the fall,[15] the following fall [i.e. a year later] they begin to grind corn again. They put the meal into twelve baskets[16] to take to the boy's house to pay for the wedding outfit."

"When is the first time they sleep together?" I asked. "The night of the morning they wash the girl's head. I forgot that." He forgot that, because, I presume, it was the ceremonial that was of significance, not the personal relationship. "I forgot that" —what more telling comment on wedding ceremonial—anywhere?

On my last visit to First Mesa I had the good luck to witness a wedding attack, the kind of mock or ceremonial attack referred to in the foregoing narrative, by the groom's father's kinswomen on his own kinswomen. High pitched voices were heard out of doors near by, about four o'clock of an afternoon, and I was called out to see the sport of the "women's fight" and join in the laughter of the neighbors standing about. There were but two women on either side, to throw water and any refuse they could pick up in the street. One woman had already had her face smeared with mud when I arrived on the scene, and all were drenched. The attackers would vociferate in shrill tones against the closed door of the house of the groom's mother—they were charging the bride with being lazy, unable to cook or to work—and then one of the women would burst out from inside to throw water and to talk back, to say that the bride *could* work, *was* industrious, etc. (No other insults appear to be indulged in on these occasions, there are, for example, no sex jeers.) But for the amused and non-interfering bystanders, two dozen or so, the row seemed thoroughly realistic. It was vigorous, though brief, lasting less than an hour.

The bride of this occasion was the sister of the town chief, the *gigyawuxti* or one of the chiefs of the houses, corresponding to the woman member of the *kyakweamosi* (chiefs of the houses) of Zuni. She had been married before and separated, as had the groom. During the ceremonial row she remained, not in the maternal house of the groom, but in her own house at Walpi. That morning she had been married by government license in the schoolhouse below the Mesa.[17] Marriage by license in the morning and in the afternoon a wedding assault, what uncritical theorizers would once have called a "rape symbol"! New custom and old, side by side, as is ever the way in Pueblo Indian life.

Although the old custom, the assault, is not a symbol of rape, since the grievance is on the part of the groom's people, his father's people against his mother's people, it is, nevertheless, we may fairly assume, given certain other data,[18] a symbol or survival of an earlier custom, that of cross-cousin marriage, where the favored or acceptable marriage was with the father's sister's daughter or clanswoman.

Notes

Originally published in *Scientific Monthly*, No. 13, 1921, pp. 259-65.

1. At Zuñi, the New Mexico pueblo where custom is most like Hopi custom, "to talk to" is also the usual expression for courting.
2. I.e., until about 4 p.m., the closing time of the Hopi work day.
3. Like the hair of Zuñi and Keresan women. Hopi women, married women, part the hair and with a string twist the locks on either side of the face.... That the Tewa women have thus preserved their own style of hairdressing is an interesting fact. Style of hairdressing and language are, as far as I know, the only distinctive traits, exclusive of religion or public ceremony, preserved by these Tewa immigrants whose town is within a stone's throw of the houses of their Hopi neighbors.
4. At Oraibi, Voth notes that all the brides of the year appear in their white blankets at the close of the *niman kachina* or farewell performance in July, the most elaborate of the masked dances. ("Oraibi Marriage Customs," p. 246. *American Anthropologist.* II. 1900).
5. Cp. Parsons, E. C. "Notes on Zuñi," pt. II, 302, 307, 322, 325. *Mem. American Anthropological Association,* IV, No. 4, 1917. Lack of weaving at present day Zuñi and the comparatively small amount there of clan cooperation would account in large part for the simpler way of getting married.
   Second marriage is among the Hopi comparatively simple because no bridal outfit is to be made.
6. Dumarest, N. "Notes on Cochiti, New Mexico," pp. 148, 149. *Mem. American Anthropological Association,* VI, No. 3, 1919.
7. On the other hand I have been told that among old-fashioned people the girl's parents and uncle (mother's brother—note the significance of participation by the uncle to the theory of cross-cousin marriage, below) would look for a boy for her. "My daughter, you will marry that boy," they would say to her. To be sure, "she might leave the boy they chose and choose her own boy," and, if her family were angry, she would go to live with some kinswoman.
8. Cp. Parsons, E. C. "Further Notes on Isleta," *American Anthropologist,* in proof.
9. This is characteristic of all invitations to clanspeople, whether to join in a work party or a name-giving rite or other ceremonial occasion. All are asked; but only the closer relatives feel any obligation to come.
10. The senior sister or cousin of the girl's father, her aunt *par excellence.*
11. At Oraibi the girl friends of the bride bring in trays of corn meal. The following morning the trays are returned filled with ears of corn by the groom's mother. ("Oraibi Marriage Customs," p. 241).
12. On Third Mesa at Oraibi the groom's head is also washed at this time, by his mother-in-law. The bodies of the couple are also bathed. The heads of bride and groom are first washed in separate bowls, then in the same bowl, a symbolic act of union, according to Voth, which has lapsed in the case of a bridegroom who has had his hair cut short at school. (Voth, H. R. "Hopi Marriage Rites on the Wedding Morning," pp. 147-9. *Brief Miscellaneous Hopi Papers.* Field Mus. Nat. Hist. Pub. 157. Anthrop. Ser:Vol. XI, No. 2, 1912). At this headwashing rite at Oraibi wrangling by the women (see above and below) is said to occur, the visiting women trying to displace the bride. ("Oraibi Marriage Customs," p. 242).
13. At Oraibi the girl's hair is taken down from the wheels or whorls worn by virgins by her own mother before mother and daughter take their first gift of meal to the boy's house ("Oraibi Marriage Customs," p. 240). The two rolls of the married woman's hair are wrapped with brown yarn stiffened with grease, so that the hair slips in and out of the wrapping or rather casing.

14. Voth got the impression at Oraibi that any townsman might join in the spinning. ("Oraibi Marriage Customs," pp. 243-244).

15. Fall or winter is the usual season for weddings ("Oraibi Marriage Customs," p. 240). None would marry in *Kyamuye*, the dangerous moon, i.e. our December.

16. The flat gayly colored baskets got in trade from Second Mesa.... At the time of my November visit, a year after Butterfly's wedding, her family had acumulated only eight baskets and when I left they had but seven, as they gave me one.

17. Hopi converts, "Christians" as they are called, are married in the church; but the unconverted are likewise required by government to be married, in the schoolhouse.

18. See Freire-Marecco, B. "Tewa Kinship Terms from the Pueblo of Hano, Arizona," *American Anthropologist,* XVI, 286, 1914. For his paternal aunt to call a boy "our bridegroom" is also Hopi practice or joke. Another Hopi joke is that were a man to marry his father's sister's daughter (clanswoman), a certain lizard called *manana* would dart at him. Oppositely, at Laguna, children are told that if they are shy of calling certain connections by the cross-cousin terms of relationship, which is "just like saying husband or wife," the lizard will dart. The cross-cousin terms of relationship in several Pueblo tribes point to some time cross-cousin marriage. In the Hopi *boinawe*, a war dance, the girl dancers appoint the men dancers, appointing from their mother's brother's sons. As sexual license once characterized war dances, in this choice of dance partners may be seen another hint of cross-cousin mating.

Tewa Mothers and Children

Measures to promote conception and childbearing are common among the Hopi and Keres and at Zuñi; but in the Tanoan towns I have still to hear of any. Tewa women have stated positively that there was nothing for a woman wanting a child to do. Nor for a woman not wanting a child. And yet a woman of San Juan whose children were born well spaced out said that she would remark to a certain woman who had been having a child every year, "You don't have good times." There is at Santa Clara a prophylaxis against twins. A girl who passes by a dog lying down in the house or by a bow and arrow laid on the floor or a gun, will have twins; and so, as twins are not desired, the thing to do is to chase the dog out or go around him, and to go around the carelessly dropped weapons.

A pregnant woman should sweep her dust out of the door quickly, not dallying. Nor should she linger about the door, going in or out. She should not start to go out and then not go. Should she behave in these ways, not sweep quickly or go out promptly, the unborn child will start out and then draw back or take a long time to come out. (San Juan). Similarly, were the prospective mother to peep out of door or window the baby would "look out [on the world] and go back." (Santa Clara).

A pregnant woman will carry a key or a stone in her belt, something hard, "so the Moon won't eat the baby." The moon in eclipse is thought to eat the unborn child, causing deformities of mouth or foot or hand. A certain San Juan man was born without toes, because, they say, the Moon ate his foot. Another man has no finger nails, and again they say the Moon ate his nails. So at eclipse, "when the Moon dies,"[1] they tell a woman not to go outdoors. (San Juan). That night she should not sleep much. Her mother should watch for her, going out to see "when the Moon is alive again." It is only the night of eclipse that, at Santa Clara, the prospective mother carries something, a key or ring, in her belt.

There is no albinism among the Tewa, and so no theory of it. There are no pregnancy taboos on the father, as elsewhere in Pueblo circles.

Eight or nine times before the birth the expectant mother bathes every four days; after the birth she bathes on the fourth day, on the eighth, on the twelfth, etc. That Mexican women do not bathe for a month after the birth seems strange to the Tewa women, and more than questionable.

During the first half of the month after the birth some women drink water that has been boiled;[2] then, during the second half, water that has been warmed only. Other women drink cold water only. During all this time watermelon and peaches are not eaten, "because, they say, they are cold."[3] Women are supposed not to sleep with their husband for one month after the birth of a daughter, for forty days after that of a son.

The mother lies in three days; on the fourth day she is up,[4] and the infant is named. The attendant aunts, maternal or paternal, give names— "the *kaiye* (mother's older sister, San Juan) or *ko'o* (mother's younger sister) will give a name, the *ki'i* (father's sister), too." One of these women, the *ki'i*, who becomes the *tsitsayiya* or navel mother, will carry the baby out at sunrise. The mother goes too.[5] Both women turn around four times, in anti-sunwise circuit. Another woman, *kaiye* or *ko'o*, goes along, carrying a fire stick and a broom. A circular sweep is made with the broom and a cutting or slicing motion (*peri*, blow as the wind does, which is exorcism for both mother and infant) and the fire stick is cast away. The baby is then carried indoors and bathed all over by the navel mother, and she and each visiting kinswoman give a name. In the bath-water is placed a fetish-stone or shell, *oga*, a cowrie shell; or *tinini*, an *olivella* shell; or *twiowénu ku*, lightning stone, *i.e.*, an arrow or spear point; or *kayé*, as are called the fetichistic stone images of bear or mountain-lion. The navel mother takes a mouthful of the water from an abalone shell and with the water still in her mouth breathes in along the corn ear, *kuliohatsiperi* (*ku*, corn; *lio'?*, *ha*, heart; *tsiperi*, blow) the rite is called. Then the ear is waved in the six directions; and the navel mother ejects the water from her mouth into the mouth of the infant. This rite is repeated for the second ear of corn. Then the navel mother breathes out on the infant. The third woman in the sunrise group repeats the whole ritual. It is the navel mother who furnishes the bowl, the fetich stone, and the two ears of corn... They thank the aunts, and give them stew and bread to take home. The two ears of corn used in naming (*kuriohatsipe*) are left on either side of the infant for ten or twelve days, "*kudionyima*, corn-taking-care-of-baby." This corn, of which the ear is completely kernelled, is planted the year following. Such completely kernelled ears (*kukayee*), which are sacrosanct, are used so that the baby will grow up perfect like the corn ear.[6]

In case a member of the curing society (*pu'fona*) is called in for a difficult delivery, the infant is named by the *pu'fona* or doctor.

These naming practices are those of San Juan. At Santa Clara the use of shell or fetich stone in the bath water appeared to be unfamiliar, and the corn ears are left alongside the infant for but four days. Of the practices in San Ildefonso and the other Mexicanised towns I got but meagre account.

In all the towns there is also a Catholic christening. Within a week or two of the birth the infant is taken to church "for his Mexican name," by his *madrinha* or *popyiya* (wet head mother) and his *padrinho* or *popotara* (wet head father). The same persons continue to serve as Catholic godparents to a family unless a godchild dies, when new godparents are called for. Possibly a like rule holds for the "navel mother" in the native ritual.

The placenta is thrown into the river.[7] For a girl, after the cord dries up and drops off, it is buried very deep near the grinding stone, so that when she grows up she will not be lazy; for a boy, it is buried in the field, "so he could work."[8]

If the navel "waters," dust from the rafters is rubbed on. Between sore navel and snake bite there is no association as in other pueblos. The mother of an infant with sore navel will not eat eggs or beans.

Santa Clara children "playing mother," 1935. Photograph by Harold Kellogg. This is one of many images of Pueblo mothers and children used by Harold and Delaine Kellogg in their children's book, Indians of the Southwest *(1936). Courtesy of the Museum of New Mexico, Negative no. 59314.*

Were a menstruating woman to hold a baby it would make the baby's skin rough and spotty, and the baby, irritable. "I wonder why the baby cries so?" somebody might ask. "Because of so-and-so, she was menstruating," somebody might answer. So no woman during menstruation is allowed to carry a baby. Lard and powder are used to allay the irritation of the skin.

I heard of a woman in confinement who had not enough milk for her infant. She wanted medicine, but nobody knew what to give her. "We used to know, but we don't know now," a comment, familiar in other connections also, on the disintegration of tribal culture of which the people are frequently aware.

To make a child able to talk early one may put a stirring stick (*wipe*), still warm from use, into his mouth and stir it around. The stirring circuit shown by my informant was anti-sunwise. (This cook stick is used in making *sa'kawe*, which is flour stirred with milk or chili). The practice, familiar elsewhere, of holding a mocking bird to the child's mouth to induce the gift of tongues was unfamiliar at San Juan.

Sick infants or children are "given," as among the Hopi,[9] to one or another of the ceremonial organisations. The present Winter Chief at Santa Clara was thus given to the Winter People's ceremonial group when he was sick in boyhood. Now and again, boy babies were vowed by their mothers to the *kwirano* of San Juan; the practice is lapsing. The *kossa* or clowns of Santa Clara are recruited also by dedication in sickness or even before birth.

The first teeth are thrown to the Sun. A child may say, "Mother, I took my tooth out." The mother will rejoin, "Keep it until to-morrow morning and let me give it to the Sun, so he will give you a new one." At sunrise the mother takes the tooth out and throws it to the Sun, asking him to give a new tooth. When the next tooth erupts, the child will say, "Mother, the Sun has given me a new tooth."

Tsabiyu[10] is the children's bugaboo. "*Tsabiyu* will come to whip you or to take you," the old people will say to a refractory child, or to a crying child; "*Tsabiyu* will hear you from *k'osena*," his home in the eastern mountains. And a child may be told that *Tsabiyu* has said that he has ears in the chimney.[11] "Knock and I will come," says he. So to a crying child or to a lazy one, a mother might say, "I am going to knock on the chimney." "Don't do it, mother," begs the child. The mother may go so far as to pick up a stick to tap with. When it looks like snow in the eastern mountains, people say to the children, "*Tsabiyu* is coming;" or, after snowing, they say, "*Tsabiyu* is under the snow, he won't come." At the Christmastide dances *Tsabiyu* actually does appear. There are two of him, one a man of the Winter People, wearing a white shirt and in white mask; the other, a man of the Summer People, in yellow shirt and black mask. Over their

Santa Clara bread baking, ca. 1935. Photograph by T. Harmon Parkhurst. Courtesy of the Museum of New Mexico, Negative no. 4147.

Grinding corn, San Juan Pueblo, 1935 (cover photo). Photograph by T. Harmon Parkhurst. Courtesy of the Museum of New Mexico, Negative no. 3971.

mask, a wig, and under it, a collar of foxskin. They wear trousers and shoes, and carry a horsewhip and a sack. They chase the children, and they visit from house to house to collect bread for their sack.[12] As early as November people begin to tell the children that *Tsabiyu* is getting ready his sack in the mountains.

Parents may punish directly, too. "Do what the old people tell you, else I will beat you," a mother might say to a child. And formerly no child would ever think of saying, as children say to-day, "What you pay me?" to a senior asking service. I heard of a man who did whip his two little boys when they had been "mean" to their sister. She and her brothers would be sent to the river, as used to be the practice, to wash their face, in winter through the ice, and on their way the brothers would tease— "boys are mean to girls."

Formerly, boys were not allowed to smoke before marrying or before going out to fight. "Why do you want to smoke? Have you killed a coyote (*i.e.*, Navajo)?" a youth might be asked.

The Santa Clara woman who opined that boys were mean to girls, and men, sometimes, to women—she had described her first husband as "an awful mean man"—this woman, now middle-aged, as a girl had learned to make pottery from an aunt who was a particularly good potter. The girl would visit her aunt and work with her. In craftsmanship, as in education at large, the Pueblo way is the way of apprenticeship.

Notes

Originally published in *Man*, No. 112, October 1924, pp. 148-51. The original footnote symbols have been converted to numerals and numbered consecutively as endnotes.

1. "The Sun dies" is said of solar eclipse, as elsewhere.
2. This is a practice of the Tewa of First Mesa also. *See* MAN, 1921, **58**.
3. Cp. MAN, 1921, **58**.
4. The day of birth is counted and the day of getting up. Were the birth on a Friday, the mother would get up on Monday.
5. Unless she happen to be a Mexican. A case was cited of naming the child of a San Juan man and a Mexican woman behind the mother's back. The paternal relatives waited until the Mexican mother was engaged in taking the customary bath at the end of her month's confinement, then, unknown to her, they named the baby. (A striking illustration of Pueblo Indian secretive tenacity!) In another case, the child did not get her Indian name until she was two and a half years old. This, too, was given surreptitiously (by her father's mother's brother's wife).... "We always hide things from Mexicans because they are mean."
6. Cp. Laguna, MAN, 1919, **86**. According to Cushing (unpublished MS.) an ear of corn, completely kernelled and white, is left alongside the Zuñi boy baby, and a dark, flat (*i.e.* branching at the top) ear, alongside the girl baby. Recently I saw a new born boy baby at Zuñi lying on his hot sand bed, with an ear of white corn on either side. This is the Hopi practice also. *See* MAN, 1921, **58**.
7. Cp. for Laguna practice, MAN, 1919, **86**.
8. Cp. for Laguna practice, MAN, 1919, **86**.
9. *See* MAN, 1921, **58**.
10. Referred to also at San Ildefonso as *Pewa sendo* or, in Spanish, as *abuelito*, little grandfather.
11. For Hopi, cp. MAN, 1921, **58**.
12. Like the Zuñi *atoshle*.